THE BOOK OF PF

THE BOOK OF PF

A No-Nonsense Guide to the OpenBSD Firewall

by Peter N.M. Hansteen

**NO STARCH
PRESS**

San Francisco

THE BOOK OF PF. Copyright © 2008 by Peter N.M. Hansteen.

 Printed on recycled paper in the United States of America

11 10 09 08 07   1 2 3 4 5 6 7 8 9

ISBN-10: 1-59327-165-4
ISBN-13: 978-1-59327-165-7

Publisher: William Pollock
Production Editor: Megan Dunchak
Cover and Interior Design: Octopod Studios
Developmental Editor: Adam Wright
Technical Reviewer: Henning Brauer
Copyeditor: Linda Recktenwald
Compositor: Riley Hoffman
Proofreader: Alina Kirsanova
Indexers: Karin Arrigoni and Peter N.M. Hansteen

For information on book distributors or translations, please contact No Starch Press, Inc. directly:

No Starch Press, Inc.
555 De Haro Street, Suite 250, San Francisco, CA 94107
phone: 415.863.9900; fax: 415.863.9950; info@nostarch.com; www.nostarch.com

Library of Congress Cataloging-in-Publication Data

Hansteen, Peter N. M.
   The book of PF : a no-nonsense guide to the OpenBSD firewall / Peter N.M. Hansteen.
       p. cm.
   Includes index.
   ISBN-13: 978-1-59327-165-7
   ISBN-10: 1-59327-165-4
 1. OpenBSD (Electronic resource) 2. TCP/IP (Computer network protocol) 3. Firewalls (Computer security) I. Title.
 TK5105.585.H385 2008
 005.8--dc22

                                                   2007042929

To Gene Scharmann,
who all those years ago nudged me in the direction of free software

BRIEF CONTENTS

CONTENTS IN DETAIL

4
WIRELESS NETWORKS MADE EASY   33

5
BIGGER OR TRICKIER NETWORKS   45

6
TURNING THE TABLES FOR PROACTIVE DEFENSE   67

7
QUEUES, SHAPING, AND REDUNDANCY   87

8
LOGGING, MONITORING, AND STATISTICS   107

9
GETTING YOUR SETUP JUST RIGHT   121

A
RESOURCES
135

B
A NOTE ON HARDWARE SUPPORT
141

INDEX
147

FOREWORD

OpenBSD's PF packet filter has enjoyed a lot of success and attention since it was first released in OpenBSD 3.0 in late 2001. While you'll find out more about PF's history in this book, in a nutshell, PF happened because it was needed by the developers and users of OpenBSD. Since the original release, PF has evolved greatly and has become the most powerful free tool available for firewalling, load balancing, and traffic managing. When PF is combined with CARP and pfsync, PF lets system administrators not only protect their services from attack, but it makes those services more reliable by allowing for redundancy and it makes them faster by scaling them using pools of servers managed through PF and hoststated.

While I have been involved with PF's development, I am first and foremost a large-scale user of PF. I use PF for security, to manage threats both internal and external, and to help me run large pieces of critical infrastructure in a redundant and scalable manner. This saves my employer (the University of Alberta, where I wear the head sysadmin hat by day) money, both in terms of downtime and in terms of hardware and software. You can use PF to do the same.

With these features comes the necessary evil of complexity. For someone well versed in TCP/IP and OpenBSD, PF's system documentation is quite extensive and usable all on its own. But in spite of extensive examples in the system documentation, it is never quite possible to put all the things you can do with PF and its related set of tools front and center without making the system documentation so large that it ceases to be useful for those experienced people who need to use it as a reference.

This book bridges the gap. If you are a relative newcomer, it can get you up to speed on OpenBSD and PF. If you are a more experienced user, this book can show you some examples of the more complex applications that help people with problems beyond the scope of the typical. For several years, Peter N.M. Hansteen has been an excellent resource for people learning how to apply PF in more than just the "How do I make a firewall?" sense, and this book extends his tradition of sharing that knowledge with others. Firewalls are now ubiquitous enough that most people have one, or several. But this book is not simply about building a firewall, it is about learning techniques for manipulating your network traffic and understanding those techniques enough to make your life as a system and network administrator a lot easier. A simple firewall is easy to build or buy off the shelf, but a firewall you can live with and manage yourself is somewhat more complex. This book goes a long way toward flattening out the learning curve and getting you thinking not only about how to build a firewall, but how PF works and where its strengths can help you. This book is an investment to save you time. It will get you up and running the right way—faster, with fewer false starts and less time experimenting.

Bob Beck
Director, The OpenBSD Foundation
http://www.openbsdfoundation.org
Edmonton, Alberta, Canada

PREFACE

This is a book about building the network you need. In order to build that network, we'll dip into the topics of firewalls and related functions, starting from a little theory along with a number of examples of filtering and other network traffic directing. We'll assume that you have a basic to intermediate command of TCP/IP networking concepts and Unix administration.

All the information in this book comes with a fair warning: As in any number of other endeavors, the things we discuss can be done in *more than one way*. You should also be aware that, as with any other book about software, the world could have changed slightly or quite a bit since the book was printed.

The information in the book is as up to date and correct as we could manage at the time of writing and refers to OpenBSD version 4.2, FreeBSD 7.0, and NetBSD 4.0, with any patches available shortly before the end of September 2007.

The book is a direct descendant of a moderately popular PF tutorial. The tutorial is also the source of the following admonition, and you may be exposed to this live if you attend one of my sessions.

WARNING *This is not a HOWTO.*

This document is not intended as a precooked recipe for cutting and pasting.

Just to hammer this in, please repeat after me:

```
The Pledge of the Network Admin

This is my network.

It is mine,
or technically, my employer's;
it is my responsibility,
and I care for it with all my heart.

There are many other networks a lot like mine,

but none are just like it.

I solemnly swear

that I will not mindlessly paste from HOWTOs.
```

The point is, while the rules and configurations I show you do work (I have tested them, and they are in some way related to what has been put into production), they may very well be overly simplistic, and they are almost certain to be at least a little off and possibly quite wrong for *your* network.

Please keep in mind that this book is intended to show you a few useful things and inspire you to achieve good things.

Please strive to understand your network and what you need to do to make it better.

Please do not paste blindly from this document or any other.

About the Book and Thanks

The book is intended to be a stand-alone document to enable you to work on your machines with only short forays into man pages and occasional reference to the online and printed resources listed in Appendix A.

The manuscript started out as a user group lecture, first presented at the January 27, 2005 meeting of the Bergen [BSD and] Linux User Group (BLUG). After I had translated the manuscript into English and expanded it slightly, Greg Lehey suggested that I should stretch it a little further and present it as a half-day tutorial for the AUUG 2005 conference. After a series of tutorial revisions, I finally started working on what was to become the book version in early 2007.

The next two paragraphs are salvaged from the tutorial manuscript and still apply to this book:

> This manuscript is a slightly further developed version of a manuscript prepared for a lecture which was announced as (translated from Norwegian):

> "This lecture is about firewalls and related functions, with examples from real life with the OpenBSD project's PF (Packet Filter). PF offers firewalling, NAT, traffic control, and bandwidth management in a single, flexible, and sysadmin-friendly system. Peter hopes that the lecture will give you some ideas about how to control your network traffic the way you want—keeping some things outside your network, directing traffic to specified hosts or services, and of course, giving spammers a hard time."

Some portions of content from the tutorial (and certainly all the really useful topics) made it into this book in some form. During the process of turning this into a useful book, a number of people have offered insights and suggestions.

People who have offered significant and useful input regarding early versions of this manuscript include Eystein Roll Aarseth, David Snyder, Peter Postma, Henrik Kramshøj, Vegard Engen, Greg Lehey, Ian Darwin, Daniel Hartmeier, Mark Uemura, Hallvor Engen, and probably a few who will remain lost in my email archives until I can grep them out of there.

I would like to thank the following organizations for their kind support: the NUUG Foundation for a travel grant that partly financed my AUUG 2005 appearance; the AUUG, UKUUG, SANE, BSDCan, and AsiaBSDCon organizations for inviting me to their conferences; and finally the FreeBSD Foundation for sponsoring my trips to BSDCan 2006 and EuroBSDCon 2006.

Finally, during the process of turning the manuscript into a book, several people did amazing things that helped this book become a lot better. I am indebted to Bill Pollock and Adam Wright for excellent developmental editing; I would like to thank Henning Brauer for excellent technical review; heartfelt thanks go to Eystein Roll Aarseth, Jakob Breivik Grimstveit, Hallvor Engen, Christer Solskogen, and Jeff Martin for valuable input on various parts of the manuscript; and, finally, warm thanks to Megan Dunchak and Linda Recktenwald for their efforts in getting the book into its final shape. Special thanks are due to Dru Lavigne for making the introductions which lead to this book getting written in the first place, instead of just hanging around as an online tutorial and occasional conference material.

Last but not least, I would like to thank my dear wife, Birthe, and my daughter, Nora, for all their love and support before and during the book writing process. This would not have been possible without you.

Now, with that out of the way, we can go on to the meat of the matter.

If You Came from Elsewhere

If you are reading this because you are considering moving your setup to PF from some other system, this section is for you. Some of the more common questions are covered here, in a FAQish, question-and-answer format.

PF looks really cool. Can I run PF on my Linux machine?

In a word, no. Over the years we have seen announcements on the PF mailing list from someone claiming to have started a Linux port of PF, but at the time of writing (late 2007), nobody has claimed to have completed such a project. The main reason for this is probably that PF is developed primarily as a deeply integrated part of the OpenBSD networking stack. Even after a decade of parallel development, the OpenBSD code still shares enough fundamentals with the other BSDs[1] to make porting possible, but porting PF to a non-BSD system would require rewriting large chunks of PF itself as well as whatever integration is needed at the target side.

If you want to use PF, you need to install and run a BSD system such as OpenBSD, FreeBSD, NetBSD, or DragonFly BSD. These are all fine operating systems, but my personal favorite is OpenBSD, mainly because that is the operating system where essentially all PF development happens, and I find the developers' and the system's no-nonsense approach refreshing.

Occasionally minor changes and bug fixes trickle back to the main PF code base from the PF implementations on other systems, but the newest, most up-to-date PF code is always to be found on OpenBSD. Some of the features described in this book are available only in the most recent versions of OpenBSD; the other BSDs tend to port the latest released PF version from OpenBSD to their code bases in time for their next release.

If you are planning to run PF on FreeBSD, NetBSD, DragonFly BSD, or other systems, you should check your system's release notes and other documentation for information about which version level of PF is included.

For some basic orientation tips for Linux users to find their way in BSD network configurations, see "I know some Linux, but I need to learn some BSD. Any pointers?" below.

I know some Linux, but I need to learn some BSD. Any pointers?

The differences and similarities between Linux and BSD are potentially a large topic if you probe deeply, but if you have a reasonable command of the basics, it should not take too long for you to feel right at home in the BSD way of doing things. In the rest of this book, we will assume that you can find

---

[1] If *BSD* does not sound familiar, here is a short explanation. The acronym expands to *Berkeley Software Distribution* and originally referred to a collection of useful software developed for the Unix operating system by staff and students at the University of California, Berkeley. Over time, the collection expanded into a complete operating system, which in turn became the forerunner of a family of systems, including OpenBSD, FreeBSD, NetBSD, DragonFly BSD, and, by some definitions, even Apple's Mac OS X. For a very readable explanation of what BSD is, see Greg Lehey's "Explaining BSD" at *http://www.freebsd.org/doc/en/articles/explaining-bsd* and of course the projects' websites.

your way around the basics of BSD network configuration. So, if you are more familiar with configuring Linux or other systems than you are with BSD, it is worth noting a few points about BSD configuration:

- Linux and BSD use different conventions for naming network interfaces. Unlike the Linux convention, BSD network interfaces are not labeled eth0 and so on. Instead, the interfaces are assigned names that equal the driver name plus a sequence number. For example, older 3Com cards using the ep driver appear as ep0, ep1, and so on, while Intel Gigabit cards are likely to end up as em0, em1, and the like. Some SMC cards are listed as sn0, and so on. Quite logical, really, and you will find this system easy to get used to.

- The configuration is */etc/rc.conf*-centric. In general, the BSDs are organized to read the configuration from the file */etc/rc.conf*, which is read by the */etc/rc* script at startup. OpenBSD recommends using */etc/rc.conf.local* for local customizations, since *rc.conf* contains the default values, while FreeBSD uses */etc/defaults/rc.conf* to store the default settings, making */etc/rc.conf* the correct place to make changes. In addition, OpenBSD uses per-interface configuration files called *hostname.<if>*, where you substitute the interface name for *<if>*.

- And finally, for the purpose of learning PF, you will need to concentrate on the */etc/pf.conf* file, which will be largely your own creation.

If you need a broader and more thorough introduction to your BSD of choice, look up the operating system's documentation, including FAQs and guides, at the project's website. You can also find some suggestions for further reading in Appendix A.

Can you recommend a GUI tool for managing my PF rule set?

This book is mainly oriented toward users who edit their rule sets in their favorite text editor.[2] The sample rule sets in this book are simple enough that you probably would not get a noticeable benefit from any of the visualization options the various GUI tools are known to offer.

A rather common line of argument claims that the PF configuration files are generally readable enough that the actual need for a graphic visualization tool is significantly smaller if you are using PF than for other tools. There are, however, several GUI tools available that can edit and/or generate PF configurations, including a complete, customized build of FreeBSD called *pfsense*, which includes a sophisticated GUI rule editor.

I recommend that you work through the parts of this book that apply to your situation, and then decide if you need to use a GUI tool in order to feel comfortable running and maintaining the systems you build.

---

[2] I will not tire you with details of which text editor I use. If you are truly interested, it's fairly easy to find out, even without contacting me.

Is there a tool I can use to convert my OtherProduct® setup to a PF configuration?

The best strategy when converting network setups, including firewall setups, from one product to another is without question to go back to the specifications or policies for your network or firewall configuration, and then implement the policies using the new tool.

There are several reasons for this. Other products will inevitably have a slightly different feature set, and the existing configuration you created for OtherProduct® is likely to mirror slightly different approaches to specific problems, which do not map easily (or at all) to features in PF and related tools. Another strong reason to create a set of *documents* that contain a complete prose specification of what your setup is meant to achieve is that it is then possible to verify whether the configuration you are running in fact implements the design goals.

Having a documented policy and taking care to update it as your needs change will make your life easier. (You might start out by putting comments in your configuration file to explain the purpose of your rules.) In some corporate settings there may even be a formal requirement for a written policy.

The impulse to look for a way to automate your conversion is quite understandable and perhaps expected in a system administrator. I urge you to resist the impulse and to perform your conversion after reevaluating your business and technical needs and (preferably) after creating or updating a formal specification or policy in the process.

NOTE *Some of the GUI tools that serve as administration front ends claim the ability to output configuration files for several firewall products and could conceivably be used as conversion tools. However, this has the effect of inserting another layer of abstraction between you and your rule set, and it also puts you at the mercy of the tool author's understanding of how PF rule sets work. Once again, I recommend working through at least the relevant parts of this book before spending serious time considering an automated conversion.*

Where can I find out more?

There are several good sources of information about PF and the systems it runs on. You have already found one in this book. You can find references to a number of other printed and online resources in Appendix A.

If you have a BSD system with PF installed, consult the online manual pages (aka man pages) for information on the exact release of the software you are dealing with. Unless otherwise indicated, the information in this book refers to the world as it looks from the command line on an OpenBSD 4.2 system.

A Little Encouragement: A PF Haiku

If you are not quite convinced yet (or even if you are reading on anyway), a little encóuragement may be in order. Over the years, a good many people have said and written their bit about PF—sometimes odd, sometimes wonderful, and sometimes just downright strange.

The poem quoted below is a good indication of the level of feeling PF sometimes inspires in its users. The poem appeared on the PF mailing list in a thread that started with a message with the subject "Things pf can't do?" in May 2004. The message had been written by someone who did not have a lot of firewall experience and who consequently found it hard to get the setup he or she wanted.

This, of course, led to some discussion, with several participants saying that if PF was hard on a newbie, the alternatives were certainly not a bit better. The thread ended in the following haiku of praise from Jason Dixon, which is given intact, along with Jason's comments:[3]

```
Compared to working with iptables, PF is like this haiku:

A breath of fresh air,
floating on white rose petals,
eating strawberries.

Now I'm getting carried away:

Hartmeier codes now,
Henning knows not why it fails,
fails only for n00b.

Tables load my lists,
tarpit for the asshole spammer,
death to his mail store.

CARP due to Cisco,
redundant blessed packets,
licensed free for me.
```

Some of the concepts Jason mentions here may sound a bit unfamiliar, but if you read on, it will all make sense in a little while.

Now I'll really stop blabbering and let you go to the first chapter, which introduces you to some important networking concepts.

---

[3] Jason Dixon, on the PF email list, May 20, 2004. See *http://marc.info/?l=openbsd-pf&m=108507584013046&w=2*.

1

WHAT PF IS

You have come here because you have heard about the networking product called *PF*, and you are most likely reading this book because you want to learn what it's all about. It's probably useful to start by spending a few moments looking at the project's history in order to put things in their proper context.

OpenBSD's *Packet Filter subsystem*, which most people refer to simply by using the abbreviated form *PF*, was originally written during an episode of extremely rapid development during the northern hemisphere summer and autumn months of 2001 by Daniel Hartmeier and a number of OpenBSD developers. The result was launched as a default part of the OpenBSD 3.0 base system in December 2001.

The new firewalling software subsystem for OpenBSD was suddenly needed when Darren Reed announced to the world that IPFilter, which at that point had been rather intimately integrated in OpenBSD, was not BSD licensed after all. In fact, that wasn't quite the case: The license itself was almost a word-for-word copy of the BSD license, omitting only the right to make changes to the code and distribute the result.

The OpenBSD version of IPFilter contained quite a number of changes and customizations, which, as it turned out, were not allowed according to the license. As a result, IPFilter was removed from the OpenBSD source tree on May 29, 2001, and for a few weeks OpenBSD-current did not contain any firewalling software.

Fortunately, in Switzerland, Daniel Hartmeier was already doing some limited experiments involving kernel hacking in the networking code. He began by hooking a small function of his own into the networking stack and then making packets pass through it. After a while he began thinking about filtering. Then the license crisis happened.

The first commit of the PF code happened on Sunday, June 24, 2001 at 19:48:58 UTC.[1]

A few months of rather intense activity followed, and the version of PF released with OpenBSD 3.0 contained a rather complete implementation of packet filtering, including network address translation.

From the looks of it, Daniel Hartmeier and the other PF developers made good use of their experience with the IPFilter code. Daniel presented a paper at USENIX in 2002 with performance tests that showed that the OpenBSD 3.1 PF performed equally well or better under stress than either IPFilter on OpenBSD 3.1 or iptables on Linux.

In addition, tests were run on the original PF from OpenBSD 3.0 that showed mainly that the code had increased in efficiency from version 3.0 to version 3.1. (The article that provides the details is available from Daniel Hartmeier's website; see *http://www.benzedrine.cx/pf-paper.html.*)

This all happened several years ago, and, like the rest the world, OpenBSD and PF have both been exposed to rapid changes in hardware and network conditions since. I have not seen comparable tests performed recently, but in my own experience and in that of others, PF's filtering overhead is pretty much negligible. As one data point (mainly to illustrate that the low end is still useful), the machine that gateways between my office's network and the world is a Pentium III 450MHz with 384MB of RAM. When I've remembered to check, I've never seen the machine at less than 96 percent *idle* according to top.

The PF code naturally generated interest in the sister BSDs as well. As we mentioned earlier, PF is available as a part of the base system of OpenBSD, where it is the default packet filter. The FreeBSD project gradually adopted

---

[1] It is worth noting that the IPFilter copyright episode spurred the OpenBSD team to perform a license audit of the entire source tree and ports in order to avoid similar situations in the future. A number of potential problems were uncovered and resolved in the months that followed, resulting in the removal of a number of potential license pitfalls for everyone involved in free software development. Theo de Raadt summed up the effort in a message to the *openbsd-misc* mailing list on February 20, 2003, available among others from the MARC mailing list archives at *http://marc.info/?l=openbsd-misc&m=10457093812445&w=2.*

PF into the base system as one of three packet-filtering systems, at first as a package, starting with version 5.3. PF has also been included in NetBSD and DragonFly BSD.[2]

The main focus in this book will be on the most up-to-date PF version available in OpenBSD 4.2. We will note significant differences between that version and the ones integrated into the other systems where appropriate.

Packet Filter? Firewall? A Few Important Terms Explained

By now I have used some terms and concepts without bothering to explain them, and I'll correct that oversight shortly. PF is a *packet filter*, that is, code that inspects network packets at the protocol and port levels and then decides what to do with them. In PF's case, this code for the most part operates in kernel space, inside the network code.

PF operates in a world that consists of *packets, protocols, connections, ports,* and *services.* In the PF worldview, *interfaces, source addresses,* and *destination addresses* are relevant too, along with a few other packet and connection characteristics.

Based on where a packet is coming from or going to, which protocol or connection it is part of, and which port it is coming from or heading for, PF is able to determine where to direct the packet or to decide if it is to be let through at all. It's equally possible to direct network traffic based on packet *contents* (usually referred to as *application-level filtering*), but that's not what PF does. We will return later to some cases where PF will hand off these kinds of tasks to other software, but first let us deal with some basics.

We've already mentioned the *firewall* concept. Perhaps the most important feature of PF and similar software is its ability to identify and block traffic that you do not want to let into your local network or let out to the world outside. At some point the term *firewall* was coined, possibly in an attempt at geek humor that would also appeal to the suits. I must admit that I'm not terribly fond of the term myself, but since the concept of packet filtering is firmly connected to the firewall concept in people's minds, I will use the term *firewall* throughout this book where it makes sense.

Network Address Translation

One other concept we will be talking about quite a lot is *inner* and *outer* addresses, or *routable* and *nonroutable* addresses. At the heart of things, this concept is not directly related to firewalls or packet filtering, but because of the way the world works today, we need to touch on it.

---

[2] There is even a personal firewall product for Microsoft Windows available that claims to be based on PF. That product, called *Core Force*, is outside the scope of this book, but if you are interested, you can find further information at the Core Security website (*http://www .coresecurity.com*).

In fact, let us be very clear about this: *NAT does not a firewall make.* That is a common misconception, and if you read on you will realize both why some less well-informed people tend to believe that NAT equals firewall and vice versa and why that does not, in fact, make sense. But first, let us go back to the whys and hows.

Why the Internet Lives on a Few White Lies

The addressing terminology that we now take more or less for granted is a relic of the early 1990s. At the time, commercialization of the Internet had just started, and somebody started calculating the number of computers that would connect to the Internet if commercialization continued. The numbers were staggering.

When the Internet protocols were originally formulated, computers were usually big, expensive things that would normally serve a large number of users simultaneously, each at his or her own more or less dumb terminal. Some of these computers ran on Unix or even an early version of BSD, while others generally ran the manufacturer's proprietary system (although back then it wasn't too hard for a university or technically oriented business to get access to its operating system's source code). Some customers even produced patches, which were then integrated into later versions of the manufacturer's system.

Only universities, research institutions, and a number of companies with Pentagon contracts were allowed to connect to the network of networks that would eventually be referred to as *the Internet.* The thinking was essentially that 32-bit addresses of 4 octets (what most people think of as *bytes*, though *octet* is the more precise term) would go an extremely long way. With a 32-bit address space, it would be possible to accommodate literally millions of machines.

Fast-forward a few years, to the early 1990s, and the Internet was no longer strictly a science project financed by the US Department of Defense. The experiment was over; the early theory about a decentralized, damage-resistant network had proven possible and even practical. The world had changed enough that the commercialization of the Internet began.

Commercial ISPs started offering Internet access to consumers, and suddenly there were millions of small, inexpensive machines wanting to connect at the same time. The new users were mainly on dial-up lines, but they came in large and ever increasing numbers. The development showed every sign of continuing and even accelerating. This meant that the smart people who had made the network had some more work to do.

Internet Protocol, Version 6 on the Far Horizon

These smart people went to the root of the problem and began working on a solution based on a larger address space—since dubbed *IP version 6*, or *IPv6* for short—which uses 128-bit addresses. IPv6 is the long-term solution, designed to both replace and (to the extent possible) seamlessly interoperate with existing networks. While some proprietary systems have been slow to rise to the IPv6 challenge, the BSDs come with IPv6 support built in, thanks to code from the KAME[3] project, which has been integrated into the baseline network stack for many years. As a result, PF has had native IPv6 support from the very beginning.

Moving the entire world to a different type of network addressing was expected to take a few years, and it was decided that an interim solution was needed.[4]

The Temporary Masquerade Solution Called NAT

The temporary solution, which has been longer lived and more popular than its inventors probably intended, consists of two parts. One part is a mechanism designed to offer the rest of the world "white lies" by letting network gateways rewrite packet addresses. The other part designates some address ranges, which had been left unassigned, for use only in networks that do not communicate directly with the Internet. Thus, several different machines at separate locations could have the same local IP address but, because the address would be translated before the traffic was let out to the Internet at large, there would be no collision.

If traffic with such nonroutable addresses were to hit the Internet at large, routers seeing the traffic would have a valid reason to refuse to let the packets pass any further. After all, with source addresses in the private ranges, the packets should not be out in the public part of the Internet at all.

We call this system *network address translation (NAT)*, sometimes referred to as *IP masquerade* or something similar. The two RFCs that define the whats and hows of this are dated 1994 (RFC 1631) and 1996 (RFC 1918), respectively.[5]

There may be a number of reasons to use the so-called RFC 1918 addresses, but traditionally and historically, the main reason has been that official addresses are either not available or not practical. RFC 1918 provided the final part of the puzzle for the interim solution to the IP address shortage, with specific ranges of IP addresses allocated to internal networks for network administrators to keep track of. With the NAT mechanism in place at the gateway, the crisis appeared to be over. The key was translation, which lets packets flow freely with minimal restriction.

---

[3] To quote the project home page at *http://www.kame.net*, "The KAME project was a joint effort of six companies in Japan to provide a free stack of IPv6, IPsec, and Mobile IPv6 for BSD variants." The main research and development activities were considered complete in March 2006, with only maintenance activity continuing, now that the important parts have been incorporated into the relevant systems.

[4] In fact, the migration is far from complete, partly due to some IPv6 design decisions that remain controversial because of possible security implications. Matters turned slightly worse when some rather serious security issues were discovered early in 2007 that are direct consequences of the IPv6 design. Just how damaging these issues will be to IPv6 adoption is still not clear at the time of writing.

[5] The two documents are RFC 1631, "The IP Network Address Translator (NAT)," dated May 1994, and RFC 1918, "Address Allocation for Private Internets," dated February 1996. See Appendix A for more information and other references.

NOTE *I keep running into people who believe that you cannot have packet filtering without NAT or that NAT provides all the network security anyone needs. Neither of these assertions is true, as you will see if you keep reading this book or other useful networking literature. See Appendix A for more information and other references.*

PF Today

At this point, we have covered a bit of background. Some years have passed since 2001, and the PF code has been through a number of revisions. Some of these revisions have introduced major new features, while others have been introduced maybe to stabilize or optimize PF. PF in its present OpenBSD 4.2 form is a mature and stable packet filter that is capable of doing quite a few things, if you want it to.

- PF classifies packets based on address family, protocol, source or destination port or port ranges, packet type, and source or destination address. It will even classify packets relative to specific interfaces or interface groups and, with a reasonable degree of certainty, based on the source operating system and a number of other parameters.

- PF can also direct traffic to destinations other than those designated by the sender—for example, to a different machine, to a program for further processing, or to a daemon listening on a port, either locally or on a different machine. (In Chapter 3 and Chapter 6 we will walk through a few sample setups where such external programs perform specific services and interact with PF in various interesting ways.)

- Before PF was written, OpenBSD contained the ALTQ code to handle load balancing and traffic shaping. After a while, ALTQ was integrated with PF, mainly for practical reasons.

- Even if NAT is not a required part of a packet filter, for practical reasons it's nice if the address-rewriting logic is handled somewhere nearby. Consequently, PF contains NAT logic as well.

- As a result of some years of development based on the real-world needs of network administrators, this powerful toolset is yours to configure via a single, essentially human-readable configuration file, */etc/pf.conf*.

Your system probably comes with a *pf.conf* file that contains some commented-out suggestions for useful configurations, as well as a few examples in the documentation directories such as */usr/share/pf/*. These examples are useful as a reference, but we will not be using them directly in this book. Instead, over the next few chapters we will be constructing a *pf.conf* file from scratch, using an incremental, hands-on approach.

2

LET'S GET ON WITH IT

In this chapter we create a very simple setup with PF. At first, we'll deal with the simplest configuration possible: a single machine that is configured to communicate with a single network. That network could very well be the Internet.

Your two main tools for configuring PF are your favorite text editor and the pfctl command-line administration tool. In ordinary, day-to-day administration, you will edit your rule set in the */etc/pf.conf* file and then load your changes using pfctl. The pfctl application can also do a number of other things and has a *large* number of options. Some of these options we will explore over the next few chapters.

In case you are wondering, there are web interfaces available for PF administration tasks, but they are not parts of the base system. The PF developers are not hostile toward these options, but they have not yet seen a graphical interface for configuring PF that is clearly preferable to editing *pf.conf* and pfctl command lines.

Simplest Possible PF Setup on OpenBSD

If you want to enable PF at startup, you need to tell the rc system to start the service. In OpenBSD, you do this by editing or creating the file */etc/rc.conf.local* and adding this magical (yet simple) line:

```
pf=YES              # enable PF
```

In addition, it is possible to specify the file where PF will find its rules:[1]

```
pf_rules=/etc/pf.conf # specify which file contains your rules
```

At the next startup, PF will be enabled. You can verify this by looking for the PF enabled message on the console.

The */etc/pf.conf* file that comes out of a normal installation of OpenBSD, FreeBSD, NetBSD, or other PF-capable system contains a number of useful suggestions, but they're all commented out.

You do not actually need to restart your machine in order to enable PF, though. You can do it just as easily by using pfctl. And since nobody wants to reboot for no good reason, type this command to enable PF on a running system:

```
$ sudo pfctl -e
```

At this point, however, we do not have a rule set, which means PF does not actually do anything.

It is probably worth noting that if you reboot your machine at this point, the *rc* script on OpenBSD will enable a default rule set, which is in fact loaded before any of the network interfaces are enabled. This default rule set is designed as a safety measure in case your gateway boots with an invalid configuration. It lets you log in and clean up whichever syntax error caused your rule set not to load. The default rule set allows a small number of basic services: ssh from anywhere, basic name resolution, and NFS mounts.

---

[1] However, putting your configuration in a file other than the default */etc/pf.conf* is probably not worth the trouble. Using the default here lets you take advantage of a number of automatic housekeeping features, such as backing up your configuration to */var/backup* every night.

Some early versions of PF ports elsewhere neglected to bring the default rules with them. This led to some discussion on those projects' mailing lists, but by the time this book is out, they should all be in line with a sensible default rule set.

Simplest Possible PF Setup on FreeBSD

Good code travels well, and FreeBSD users will tell you that good code from elsewhere tends to find its way into FreeBSD sooner or later. PF is no exception, and from FreeBSD 5.2.1 and the late 4.*x* series onward, PF and related tools made their way into FreeBSD.

On FreeBSD, it seems that you need a little more magic in your */etc/rc.conf* file, but it's still a simple set of commands. There are some differences between the FreeBSD 4.*x* and 5.*x* and newer releases with respect to PF. Refer to the *FreeBSD Handbook*, specifically the PF chapter at *http://www.freebsd.org/doc/en_US.ISO8859-1/books/handbook/firewalls-pf.html*, to see which information applies in your case. The PF code in FreeBSD 7.0 is equivalent to the code in OpenBSD 4.1. By looking at your */etc/defaults/rc.conf* file, you will see that the defaults values for PF-related settings in FreeBSD are as follows:

```
pf_enable="NO"                  # Set to YES to enable packet filter (pf)
pf_rules="/etc/pf.conf"         # rules definition file for pf
pf_program="/sbin/pfctl"        # where the pfctl program lives
pf_flags=""                     # additional flags for pfctl
pflog_enable="NO"               # Set to YES to enable packet filter logging
pflog_logfile="/var/log/pflog"  # where pflogd should store the logfile
pflog_program="/sbin/pflogd"    # where the pflogd program lives
pflog_flags=""                  # additional flags for pflogd
pfsync_enable="NO"              # Expose pf state to other hosts for syncing
pfsync_syncdev=""               # Interface for pfsync to work through
pfsync_ifconfig=""              # Additional options to ifconfig(8) for pfsync
```

The only ones that you actually need to add to your configuration are these:

```
pf_enable="YES"     # Enable PF (load module if required)
pflog_enable="YES"  # start pflogd(8)
```

On FreeBSD, PF is compiled as a kernel-loadable module by default. This means that you can start PF with

```
$ sudo kldload pf
```

followed by

```
$ sudo pfctl -e
```

The pfctl -e command should produce the following output:

```
No ALTQ support in kernel
ALTQ related functions disabled
pf enabled
```

Assuming you have put the relevant lines in your */etc/rc.conf,* you could also use the PF rc script to operate PF. Use

```
$ sudo /etc/rc.d/pf start
```

to enable PF, or use

```
$ sudo /etc/rc.d/pf stop
```

to disable the packet filter. The PF rc script supports a few other operations as well. However, it is worth noting that at this point we still do not have a rule set. Again, since we haven't gotten around to writing an actual rule set, PF is not actually doing anything—it's just passing packets.

Simplest Possible PF Setup on NetBSD

On NetBSD 2.0 and newer, PF is available as a loadable kernel module that can be installed via packages (*security/pflkm*) or compiled into a static kernel configuration. In NetBSD 3.0 onward, PF is part of the base system.

If you want to enable PF in your kernel configuration (rather than loading the kernel module), add these lines to your kernel configuration:

```
pseudo-device  pf        # PF packet filter
pseudo-device  pflog     # PF log interface
```

In */etc/rc.conf* you need the lines

```
lkm="YES" # do load kernel modules
pf=YES
pflogd=YES
```

to enable loadable kernel modules, PF, and the PF log interface, respectively.

If you installed the module, load it with

```
$ sudo modload /usr/lkm/pf.o
```

followed by

```
$ sudo pfctl -e
```

to enable PF.

Alternatively, you can run the rc scripts

```
$ sudo /etc/rc.d/pf start
```

to enable PF and

```
$ sudo /etc/rc.d/pflogd start
```

to enable the logging.

To load the module automatically at startup, add the following line to */etc/lkm.conf*:

```
/usr/lkm/pf.o - - - - - AFTERMOUNT
```

If everything is still correct at this point, you are ready to create your first PF rule set.

First Rule Set—A Single, Stand-Alone Machine

This is the simplest possible setup: a single machine that will not run any services, talking to only one network (which may be the Internet).

For now, we will use a */etc/pf.conf* file that looks like this:

```
block in all
pass out all keep state
```

This rule set denies any incoming traffic, allows traffic we make ourselves, and retains state information on our connections. That's the way rules are evaluated in PF configurations: The rules are read from top to bottom, and the *last* rule in your rule set that matches for the packet or connection is the one that will be applied. That's all you need to know about the matter at this point. We will be looking at evaluation order later when the rule sets grow a bit longer than the one we have here.

The keep state part of the rule tells PF that when a connection matches the rule, we want to let the return traffic for connections matching that rule pass back in the other direction, too. In order to achieve that, we keep information about the connection as an entry in the *state table*. This information includes various counters and sequence numbers, which are normally quite useful. We can instruct PF to act on state information in various ways, but in a simple case like this, the main purpose is to let return traffic for the connections we initiate pass back to us.

It is worth noting that from OpenBSD 4.1 onward, the default for pass rules is to keep state information,[2] so the equivalent rule set in the new style is even simpler:

```
# minimal rule set, OpenBSD 4.1 onward keeps state by default
block in all
pass out all
```

In fact, you could even leave out the all keyword here if you like. The other BSDs are likely to pick up the new defaults soon, and for the rest of this book we will be sticking to the newer-style rules, with an occasional reminder in case you are using an older-style system.

It goes pretty much without saying that passing all traffic generated by a specific host implies a great deal of trust that the host in question is, in fact, trustworthy. This is something you do only if this is a machine you know you can trust.

If you are ready to use the rule set, load it with

```
$ sudo pfctl -ef /etc/pf.conf
```

The rule set should load with no error messages or warnings. On all but the slowest systems, you will be returned to the $ prompt immediately.

TESTING THE RULE SET

Even with a simple two-line rule set like this, you can usefully test whether or not the rule set works as expected.

Testing to see if your configuration conforms to your expectations is always a good idea, and proper testing will become even more essential once you move on to more complicated configurations. Writing a test case for each change you make to the rule set, complete with the results you expect to see, is a *best practice*, and the sooner you get into the habit, the better.

For the rule set we have here, you could test something basic like name resolution by checking the output of $ host nostarch.com, which should return information such as the IP address of the host *nostarch.com* and the hostnames of the domain's email exchangers. If you have ssh access to another system, see if you can complete a login and run commands on the remote system. You could also surf the Web (on OpenBSD, lynx is in the base system).

Basically any service you try to access from your own system should work, and any service you try to access on your system from anywhere else should produce a Connection refused message.

---

[2] In fact, the new default corresponds to keep state flags S/SA, ensuring that only initial SYN packets during connection setup create state, eliminating some puzzling error scenarios. If you want to filter statelessly, you can specify no state for the rules where you do not want to record or keep state information. On FreeBSD, OpenBSD 4.1–equivalent PF code was merged into version 7.0.

Slightly Stricter, with Lists and Macros

The first rule set was an extremely simple example, and even though we could use it to demonstrate some basics about how networks and packet filtering work, it is probably too simplistic for practical use. For a slightly more structured and complete setup, we can construct a slightly more realistic example. However, this rule set is still based on the single, stand-alone system that connects to one network.

In this configuration, we'll start by denying everything and then allowing only those things we know that we need.[3] This gives us the opportunity to introduce two of the features that make PF such a wonderful tool: lists and macros.

We'll make some changes to */etc/pf.conf*, starting with

```
block all
```

This is a little more restrictive than the first rule set we used. The new rule blocks all traffic in both directions, incoming and outgoing. This is the sensible default and one you will get used to seeing. In all complete rule sets we develop over the next few chapters, this is the baseline filtering rule. Subsequent rules will cut your traffic some slack, but before we get to the actual rules, we need to make a few more changes at the very top of the configuration file. We need to define some macros so we can use them later in the rule set:

```
tcp_services = "{ ssh, smtp, domain, www, pop3, auth, https, pop3s }"
udp_services = "{ domain }"
```

Here we've demonstrated several things. You now know what macros look like, and we've shown that macros may be lists. You probably also expected to see port numbers by now, but as we have shown here, PF understands rules using service names as well as port numbers. The names are the ones listed in your */etc/services* file.

This gives us something to put in our rules, which we edit slightly to look like this:

```
block all
pass out proto tcp to any port $tcp_services
pass proto udp to any port $udp_services
```

NOTE *Please remember to add* keep state *to these rules if your system has a PF version older than OpenBSD 4.1.*

---

[3] You may ask why I write the rule set to default deny. The short answer is that it gives you better control at the expense of some thinking. The point of packet filtering is to take control, not to play catch-up with what the bad guys do. Marcus Ranum has written a very entertaining and informative article about this called "The Six Dumbest Ideas in Computer Security," which comes highly recommended. It is available at *http://www.ranum.com/security/computer_security/editorials/dumb/index.html* and is a very good read.

The strings $tcp_services and $udp_services are macro references. Macros are expanded in place when the rule set loads, and the running rule set will have the full lists inserted where the macros are referenced. Macros are extremely good for readability. Even in a small rule set like this, the rules are easier to grasp and maintain than if we had dealt with the full list or port numbers.

This is the point where you pick up the habit of always looking for parts of your rule set that could reasonably be written as macros to help readability. As your rule sets expand, you will be happy that you did.

You may be thinking about how UDP is stateless and connectionless, but PF creates and maintains data equivalent to state information for UDP traffic in order to ensure that UDP return traffic is allowed back in. One common example where state information for UDP is useful is for handling name resolution. When you ask a nameserver to resolve a domain name to an IP address or to resolve an IP address back to a hostname, it is quite reasonable to assume that you want to receive the answer. Retaining state information or the functional equivalent about your UDP traffic makes this possible.

Since we've made changes to our *pf.conf* file, we must load the new rules:

```
$ sudo pfctl -f /etc/pf.conf
```

If there are no syntax errors, pfctl will not output any messages during the rule load.

It is worth noting that you can use the -v flag to produce more verbose pfctl output:

```
$ sudo pfctl -vf /etc/pf.conf
```

In this specific case it probably will not make a difference, however. If there are no errors in your rule set, pfctl will not produce any output before returning you to the command-line prompt.

If you have made extensive changes to your rule set, you may want to check the rules before attempting to load them. The command to do this is pfctl -nf /etc/pf.conf. The -n option causes the rules to be interpreted only without loading the rules. This gives you an opportunity to correct any errors. If pfctl finds any syntax errors in your rule set, it will exit with an error message that points out the line number where the error occurred.

Under any circumstances, unless you *flushed* your rules (using pfctl -F and some specifier) before attempting to load new rules from your configuration file, the last valid rule set loaded will be in force until you either disable PF or load a new rule set. The way rule set loading works, pfctl syntax checks and then loads your new rule set completely before switching over to the new one. With a valid rule set loaded, there is no intermediate state with a partial rule set or no rules loaded. The upshot of this is that flushing the rule set is rarely a good idea, since it effectively puts your packet filter in a pass all mode.

Statistics from pfctl

The tests you just performed showed that PF was running and hopefully that your rules behaved as expected. However, in other circumstances you may want to check that PF is actually running and review statistics about its activity. In addition to enabling and disabling PF and loading rule sets, the `pfctl` program offers many different types of information displays. To access these features, you use `pfctl -s`, adding the type of information you want to display.

The following example was taken from my home gateway while I was working on this book:

```
$ sudo pfctl -s info
Status: Enabled for 17 days 00:24:58        Debug: Urgent

Interface Stats for ep0              IPv4               IPv6
  Bytes In                     9257508558                  0
  Bytes Out                     551145119                352
  Packets In
    Passed                        7004355                  0
    Blocked                         18975                  0
  Packets Out
    Passed                        5222502                  3
    Blocked                            65                  2

State Table                          Total               Rate
  current entries                       15
  searches                        19620603            13.3/s
  inserts                           173104             0.1/s
  removals                          173089             0.1/s
Counters
  match                             196723             0.1/s
  bad-offset                             0             0.0/s
```

fragment	22	0.0/s
short	0	0.0/s
normalize	0	0.0/s
memory	0	0.0/s
bad-timestamp	0	0.0/s
congestion	0	0.0/s
ip-option	28	0.0/s
proto-cksum	325	0.0/s
state-mismatch	983	0.0/s
state-insert	0	0.0/s
state-limit	0	0.0/s
src-limit	26	0.0/s
synproxy	0	0.0/s

The first line here indicates that PF is enabled and has been running for a little more than two weeks, which is equal to the time since I last upgraded to the latest snapshot (yes, at that time my home gateway ran OpenBSD-current). The information here is roughly in line with the statistics you should expect to see on the gateway for a small network configured for IPv4 only.[4]

At this point, you probably want to spend some time exploring pfctl and your configuration. As we hinted earlier, pfctl is a powerful program that supports a large number of options. For example, pfctl -s all provides highly detailed information about PF on your system. Try it and have a look. While you're there, look into some of the other pfctl options. The command man 8 pfctl gives you full information.

With the last rule set, you have a single machine that should be able to communicate rather well with other Internet-connected machines. This very basic rule set serves as a useful starting point for taking control of your network traffic. One of the most important underlying themes in this book is about being in control. In many ways, the rest of this book is about extending your rule set to fit your network needs while remaining firmly in control of what goes on in your networks.

A few things are still missing, though. You will probably want to add rules that let at least some ICMP and UDP traffic through—for your own trouble-shooting needs, if nothing else.

Looking forward, you should start to think about network services that have consequences for your security, such as ftp. Even though more modern and more secure options are available, more likely than not, you will be required to handle these types of services. You may not have to do that now, on the stand-alone personal system, but once you get around to setting up a gateway for a network with more people and more computers, these consequences will become important.

Using packet filtering intelligently to handle services that are demanding security-wise is a recurring theme in this book.

---

[4] Do not be alarmed by the three packets passed and two blocked in the IPv6 column. OpenBSD comes with IPv6 built in, and during network interface configuration, the TCP/IP stack sends IPv6 neighbor solicitation requests for the link local address by default. In a normal IPv4-only configuration, only the first few packets actually pass, and by the time our PF rule set is fully loaded, the last two IPv6 packets are blocked by our block all default rule.

3

INTO THE REAL WORLD

In the previous chapter we demonstrated the configuration for basic packet filtering on a single machine. In this chapter we'll build on that basic setup but move into more conventional territory: the packet-filtering gateway. While most of the items in this chapter are potentially useful in a single-machine setup, our main focus now is to set up a gateway that handles common network services.

A Simple Gateway, NAT If You Need It

At this point we will start building what you probably associate with the term *firewall*: a machine that acts as a gateway for at least one other machine. In addition to forwarding packets between its various networks, this machine's mission will be to improve the signal-to-noise ratio in the network traffic it handles. That's where our PF configuration comes in.

However, before diving into the practical configuration details, we need to dip into some theory. Bear with me; this will end up saving you some of the headaches I've seen discussed on mailing lists and newsgroups all too often.

Gateways and the Pitfalls of in, out, and on

In the single-machine setup, life is relatively simple. Traffic you create should either pass out to the rest of the world or get blocked by your filtering rules, and you decide what you want to let in from elsewhere.

When you set up a gateway, your perspective changes. You go from the *It's me versus the network out there* mindset to *I am the one who decides what to pass to or from all the networks I am connected to.* The machine has several, or at least two, network interfaces, each connected to a separate network.

Now, it's very reasonable to think that if you want traffic to pass from the network connected to re1 to hosts on the network connected to re0, you will need a rule like

```
pass in proto tcp on re1 from re1:network to re0:network port $ports keep state
```

which keeps track of states as well.[1]

However, one of the most common and most complained-about mistakes in firewall configuration is not realizing that the to keyword does not in itself guarantee passage all the way there.

The rule we just wrote only lets the traffic pass in *to* the gateway itself, on the specific interface named in the rule.

To let the packets get a bit farther and move on to the next network over, you would need a matching rule that says something like

```
pass out proto tcp on re0 from re1:network to re0:network port $ports keep state
```

This rule will work, but it will not necessarily achieve what you want. In fact, this rule only lets packets with a destination in the network directly connected to re0 pass, nothing else.

If there are good reasons why you need to have rules that are this specific in your rule set, you'll know you need them and why. By the time you have worked through to the end of the book (or probably a bit earlier), you should be able to articulate with some precision just when such rules are needed. However, for the basic gateway configurations we will be dealing with in this chapter, it is likely that you will want to write rules that are not interface specific. In fact, in some cases it is not really useful to specify direction, either. What you probably want to use is a rule that says

```
pass proto tcp from re1:network to any port $ports keep state
```

---

[1] In fact, even if the keep state part denotes the default behavior and is redundant if you are working with OpenBSD 4.1 or equivalent, there is generally no need to remove the specification from your rules when upgrading your rule set from earlier versions. To ease transition, the examples in this book will make this distinction when needed.

to let your local net access the Internet and leave the detective work to the antispoof and scrub code. (They are both pretty good, and we will get back to them later.) For now, we just accept the fact that for simple setups, interface-bound in and out rules are likely to add more clutter than they are worth to your rule sets.

For a busy network admin, a readable rule set is a safer rule set.

For the remainder of this book, with some exceptions, we will keep the rules as simple as possible for readability. There are cases where we need to specify direction and interface, and we will be returning to some such cases later in the book.

What Is Your Local Network, Anyway?

Earlier in this chapter we introduced the interface:network notation. It's a nice piece of shorthand, but you can make your rule set even more readable and maintainable by taking the macro a tiny bit further.

For example, you could define a $localnet macro as the network directly attached to your internal interface (re1:network in the examples above).

Alternatively, you could change the definition of $localnet to an IP address/netmask notation to denote a network, such as 192.168.100.0/24 for a subnet of private IPv4 addresses or fec0:dead:beef::/64 for an IPv6 range.

If your network requires it, you could even define your $localnet as a list of networks. Whatever your specific needs, a sensible $localnet definition and a typical pass rule of the type

```
pass proto { tcp, udp } from $localnet to any port $ports
```

could end up saving you a few headaches. We will stick to that convention from here on.

Setting Up

We assume that the machine has acquired another network card, or at any rate, you have set up a network connection from your local network to one or more additional networks, via Ethernet, PPP, or other means.

In our context it is not very interesting to look at the details of how the interfaces get configured. We do need to know that the interfaces are up and running, though.

For the discussion and examples that follow, only the interface names will differ between a PPP setup and an Ethernet one, and we will do our best to get rid of the actual interface names as quickly as possible.

First, we need to turn on gatewaying in order to let the machine forward the network traffic it receives on one interface to other networks via a separate interface. Initially we will do this on the command line with a sysctl command; for traditional IPv4 it is as follows:

```
# sysctl net.inet.ip.forwarding=1
```

If we need to forward IPv6 traffic, the sysctl command is

```
# sysctl net.inet6.ip6.forwarding=1
```

This is fine for now, but in order for this to work once you reboot the computer at some time in the future, you need to enter these settings into the relevant configuration files.

On OpenBSD and NetBSD, you do this by editing */etc/sysctl.conf*. OpenBSD's default *sysctl.conf* has these lines commented out, and you enable them by removing the hash mark (#) from the start of the line, like this:

```
net.inet.ip.forwarding=1
net.inet6.ip6.forwarding=1
```

On NetBSD, you need to add these lines to the file if they are not there already.

Editing */etc/sysctl.conf* will work on FreeBSD too, but by FreeBSD conventions, you make the change by putting these lines in your */etc/rc.conf*:

```
gateway_enable="YES"       #for ipv4
ipv6_gateway_enable="YES" #for ipv6
```

The net effect is identical: The FreeBSD rc script sets the two values via the sysctl command. However, a larger part of the FreeBSD configuration is centralized in the *rc.conf* file.

Now it's time to check: Are all of the interfaces you intend to use up and running? Use ifconfig -a or ifconfig interface_name to find out.

The output of ifconfig -a on one of my systems looks like this:

```
peter@delilah:~$ ifconfig -a
lo0: flags=8049<UP,LOOPBACK,RUNNING,MULTICAST> mtu 33224
        groups: lo
        inet 127.0.0.1 netmask 0xff000000
        inet6 ::1 prefixlen 128
        inet6 fe80::1%lo0 prefixlen 64 scopeid 0x5
xl0: flags=8843<UP,BROADCAST,RUNNING,SIMPLEX,MULTICAST> mtu 1500
        lladdr 00:60:97:83:4a:01
        groups: egress
        media: Ethernet autoselect (100baseTX full-duplex)
        status: active
        inet 194.54.107.18 netmask 0xfffffff8 broadcast 194.54.107.23
        inet6 fe80::260:97ff:fe83:4a01%xl0 prefixlen 64 scopeid 0x1
fxp0: flags=8843<UP,BROADCAST,RUNNING,SIMPLEX,MULTICAST> mtu 1500
        lladdr 00:30:05:03:fc:41
        media: Ethernet autoselect (100baseTX full-duplex)
        status: active
        inet 194.54.103.65 netmask 0xffffffc0 broadcast 194.54.103.127
        inet6 fe80::230:5ff:fe03:fc41%fxp0 prefixlen 64 scopeid 0x2
pflog0: flags=141<UP,RUNNING,PROMISC> mtu 33224
enc0: flags=0<> mtu 1536
```

Your setup is probably at least a little different. Here, the physical interfaces on my system are xl0 and fxp0, while the logical interfaces lo0 (the loopback interface), enc0 (the encapsulation interface for IPsec use), and pflog0 (the PF logging device) are most likely there on your system, too.

If you are on a *dial-up* connection, you probably use some variant of PPP for your Internet connection, and your external interface is the tun0 pseudo-device. If your connection is via some sort of broadband connection such as ADSL, you may have an Ethernet interface to play with. However, if you are in the significant subset of ADSL users who use PPP over Ethernet (PPPoE), the correct external interface will be one of the pseudo-devices tun0 or pppoe0 (depending on whether you use userland pppoe(8) or kernel mode pppoe(4)), not the physical Ethernet interface.

Depending on your setup, you may need to do some other device-specific configuration for your interfaces. All I can say at this point is get it done so we can move on to the TCP/IP level and deal with our packet-filtering configuration.

If you still intend to allow any traffic initiated by machines on the inside, your */etc/pf.conf* could look roughly like this:

```
ext_if = "re0"  # macro for external interface - use tun0 or pppoe0 for PPPoE
int_if = "re1"  # macro for internal interface
localnet = $int_if:network
# ext_if IP address could be dynamic, hence ($ext_if)
nat on $ext_if from $localnet to any -> ($ext_if)
block all
pass from { lo0, $localnet } to any keep state
```

Note the use of macros to assign logical names to the network interfaces. Here, RealTek Gigabit Ethernet cards are used, but this is the last time we will find this to be of any interest whatsoever. In truly simple setups such as this one, we may not gain very much by using macros like these, but once the rule sets grow a little larger, you will learn to appreciate the readability this adds to the rule sets.

Also note the nat rule. This is where we handle the network address translation from the nonroutable address inside your local net to the sole official address assigned to you. If your network uses official, routable addresses, you can simply leave this line out of your configuration.

The parentheses surrounding the last part of the nat rule, ($ext_if), are there to compensate for the possibility that the IP address of the external interface may be dynamically assigned. This detail will ensure that your network traffic runs without serious interruption even if the external IP address changes.

On the other hand, this rule set probably allows more traffic than you actually want to pass out of your network. In one of the networks where I've done a bit of work, the equivalent macro is

```
client_out = "{ ftp-data, ftp, ssh, domain, pop3, auth, nntp, http,\
       https, 446, cvspserver, 2628, 5999, 8000, 8080 }"
```

with the rule

```
pass inet proto tcp from $localnet to any port $client_out
```

This may be a somewhat peculiar selection of ports, but it's exactly what the people who worked there needed at the time. Some of the numbered ports were required for specific applications. Your needs probably differ in the details, but this should cover at least some of the more useful services.

In addition, we have a few other pass rules. We will be returning to some of the more interesting ones rather soon. One pass rule that is useful to those of us who want the ability to administer our machines from elsewhere is

```
pass in inet proto tcp from any to any port ssh
```

or, if you prefer,

```
pass in inet proto tcp from any to $ext_if port ssh
```

The from any part is really quite permissive. It lets you log in from anywhere, which is great if you travel a lot and need ssh access from unknown locations around the world. If you're not all that mobile (say you haven't quite developed the taste for conferences in far-flung locations, or you really want to leave your colleagues to fend for themselves while you're on vacation), you may want to tighten up the from part to include only the places from which you and other administrators are likely to log in for legitimate business reasons.

Anyway, this very basic rule set is not complete just yet. The next thing we need to do is to make the name service work for our clients. We start with another macro at the beginning of our rule set:

```
udp_services = "{ domain, ntp }"
```

We supplement that with a rule that passes the traffic we want through our firewall:

```
pass quick inet proto { tcp, udp } to any port $udp_services
```

Note the quick keyword in this rule. We have started writing rule sets that consist of several rules, and it is time to revisit the relationships and interactions among them.

We touched on this in the previous chapter, but repeating this information does not hurt: The rules are evaluated from top to bottom, in the sequence they are written in the configuration file. For each packet or connection evaluated by PF, *the last matching rule* in the rule set is the one that is applied.

The quick keyword offers an escape from the ordinary sequence. When a packet matches a quick rule, the packet is treated according to the present rule. The rule processing stops without considering any further rules that might have matched the packet. As your rule sets grow longer and more complicated, you will find this quite handy, for example, when you need a few isolated exceptions to your general rules.

This quick rule also takes care of the Network Time Protocol (NTP), which is used for time synchronization. One fact common to both the name-service and time-synchronization protocols is that they may, under certain circumstances, communicate alternately over TCP and UDP.

Testing Your Rule Set

You may not have gotten around to writing that formal test suite for your rule sets just yet, but there is every reason to test that your configuration works as expected.

The same basic tests in the stand-alone example from the previous chapter still apply, only now you need to test from the other hosts in your network as well as from your packet-filtering gateway. For each of the services you specified in your pass rules, test that machines in your local network get meaningful results. From any machine in your local network, the output of a command like $ host nostarch.com should return exactly the same result as it did when you tested the stand-alone rule set on pages 12 and 15[2] and traffic for the services you have specified should pass.

You may not think it's necessary, but it does not hurt to check to see that the rule set works as expected from outside your gateway as well. If you have done exactly what this chapter says, it should not be possible to contact machines in your local network from the outside.

WHY ONLY IP ADDRESSES, NO HOST NAMES OR DOMAIN NAMES?

Looking at the examples up to this point, you have probably noticed that the rule sets all have macros that expand into IP addresses or address ranges, but never host names or domain names. You're probably wondering why. After all, we've seen that PF lets you use service names in your rule set, so why not host names or domain names?

The answer is, yes, you can use domain names and host names in your rule set, but then the rule set would only be valid after the name service is running and accessible. In the default configuration, PF is loaded before any network services are running. This means that if you want to use domain names and host names in your PF configuration, you will need to change the system's startup sequence (by editing /etc/rc.local, perhaps) to load the name service–dependent rule set only after the name service is available.

---

[2] Unless, of course, the information changed in the meantime. Some sysadmins are fond of practical jokes, but most of the time, changes in DNS zone information are due to real-world needs in that particular organization or network.

That Sad Old FTP Thing

The short list of real-life TCP ports we looked at on page 21 contained, among other things, FTP, the classic File Transfer Protocol. FTP is a relic of the early Internet, when experiments were the norm and security was not really on the horizon in any modern sense. FTP actually predates TCP/IP,[3] and it is possible to track the protocol's development through more than 50 RFCs. After more than 30 years, FTP is both a sad old thing and a problem child, emphatically so for anyone trying to combine FTP and firewalls. FTP is an old and weird protocol, with a lot to dislike. The most common points against it are these:

- Passwords are transferred in the clear.

- The protocol demands the use of at least two TCP connections (control and data) on separate ports.

- When a session is established, data is communicated via ports selected at random.

All of these points make for security challenges, even before considering any potential weaknesses in client or server software that may lead to security issues. As any network greybeard will tell you, these problems have been known to crop up when you need them the least.

Under any circumstances, other more modern and more secure options for file transfer exist, such as sftp or scp, which feature both authentication and data transfer via encrypted connections. Competent IT professionals should have a preference for some form of file transfer other than FTP.

Regardless of our professionalism and preferences, there are always times when we need to handle things we would prefer not to. In the case of letting FTP traffic pass through firewalls, we can still handle this by redirecting the traffic to a small program that is written specifically for this purpose. The upside for us is that handling FTP offers the first chance to look at redirection.

The easiest way to handle FTP is to have PF redirect the traffic for that service to an external application that acts as a *proxy* for the service. The proxy then interacts with your packet filter through a well-defined interface.

Depending on your configuration, which operating system you are using as the platform for your PF firewall, and how you count them, three or four different options are available for this particular task.

We will present these options in roughly chronological order according to their ages. The original, now mainly historical, FTP proxy for PF is described below in "FTP Through NAT: ftp-proxy." We'll then move on to two newer, intermediate solutions developed by Camiel Dobbelaar in "FTP, PF, and Routable Addresses: ftpsesame, pftpx, and ftp-proxy" on page 26, before finally moving on to the modern FTP proxy that was introduced in OpenBSD 3.9 in "New-Style FTP: ftp-proxy" on page 26.

---

[3] The earliest RFC describing the File Transfer Protocol is RFC 114, dated April 10, 1971. The switch to TCP/IP happened with FTP version 5, as defined in RFCs 765 and 775, dated June and December 1980, respectively.

FTP Through NAT: ftp-proxy

In November 2005, the old ftp-proxy (*/usr/libexec/ftp-proxy*) was replaced in OpenBSD-current with the new ftp-proxy, which lives in */usr/sbin*. This is the software that is included in OpenBSD 3.9 onward.

NOTE *OpenBSD 3.8 equivalents or earlier only: This section is destined to become purely historical as soon as the last PF port moves on to the newer version. If you are using a modern PF version, jump directly to "New-Style FTP: ftp-proxy" on page 26 for up-to-date information.*

The old-style ftp-proxy program, which is a part of the base system on systems with PF versions corresponding to OpenBSD 3.8 or earlier, is usually called via the inetd superserver via an */etc/inetd.conf* entry.

You may need to enable the inetd service by adding an

```
inetd_enable="YES"
```

line to your *rc.conf* and possibly adjusting other inetd-related configuration settings.

The line quoted here specifies that ftp-proxy runs in NAT mode on the loopback interface:

```
127.0.0.1:8021 stream tcp nowait root /usr/libexec/ftp-proxy ftp-proxy -n
```

This line may be in *inetd.conf* already, possibly commented out with a # character at the beginning of the line. On FreeBSD, an appropriate line with a slightly different syntax is already in your *inetd.conf*, commented out. To enable the ftp-proxy, you need to uncomment that line.

To enable your change, restart inetd.

On FreeBSD, NetBSD, and other rcNG-based BSDs, do this with

```
$ sudo /etc/rc.d/inetd restart
```

or equivalent. Consult man 8 inetd if you are unsure.

Now for the actual redirection. Redirection (rdr) rules and NAT (nat) rules fall into the same rule class. These rules may be referenced directly by other rules, and filtering rules may depend on these rules. Logically, rdr and nat rules need to be defined before the filtering rules.

We insert our rdr rule immediately after the nat rule in our */etc/pf.conf*:

```
rdr pass on $int_if proto tcp from any to any port ftp -> 127.0.0.1 port 8021
```

In addition, the redirected traffic must be allowed to pass. We achieve this with

```
pass in on $ext_if inet proto tcp from port ftp-data to ($ext_if) \
    user proxy flags S/SA keep state
```

Save your *pf.conf* file, and then load the new rules with

```
$ sudo pfctl -f /etc/pf.conf
```

At this point you will probably have users noticing that FTP works before you get around to telling them what you've done.

This example assumes you are using NAT on a gateway with nonroutable addresses on the inside. The configuration here covers the basics and should interact well with a wide range of FTP servers and clients. In practice, you may need to compensate for quirks on either side of the fence, so for the finer points of ftp-proxy configuration, do look up the various options the proxy offers. Looking at man ftp-proxy, you will find example methods for restricting the range or source ports for data connections, as well as variations on how to interact with other applications and services.

FTP, PF, and Routable Addresses: ftpsesame, pftpx, and ftp-proxy

In cases where the local network uses official, routable addresses inside the firewall, several users have reported that they had trouble making the pre–OpenBSD 3.9 ftp-proxy work properly. Back in the pre–OpenBSD 3.9 days, I struggled with it myself. After I'd already spent too much time on the problem, I was relieved to find a solution to this specific problem offered by a friendly Dutchman called Camiel Dobbelaar. His solution was a daemon called ftpsesame.

Local networks using official addresses inside a firewall are apparently rare enough that I'll skip over any further treatment. If you are running one of the PF-enabled operating systems in which the integrated PF code predates OpenBSD 3.9, keep ftpsesame in mind.

On FreeBSD, ftpsesame is available through the ports system as *ftp/ftpsesame*. Alternatively, you can download ftpsesame from Sentia at *http://www.sentia.org/projects/ftpsesame*.

Once installed and running, ftpsesame hooks into your rule set via an *anchor*, a named sub–rule set. The documentation consists of a man page with examples that you can probably simply copy and paste.

ftpsesame never made it into the base system, and Camiel went on to write a new solution to the same set of problems. The new program, at first called pftpx, is available from *http://www.sentia.org/downloads/pftpx-0.8.tar.gz* and through the FreeBSD ports system as *ftp/pftpx*. The pftpx package comes with a fairly complete and well-written man page to get you started.

A further developed version, suitably renamed as the new ftp-proxy, is now part of OpenBSD since release 3.9 as */usr/sbin/ftp-proxy*. The new ftp-proxy is described in "New-Style FTP: ftp-proxy" below.

New-Style FTP: ftp-proxy

If you are working with a PF version based on OpenBSD 3.9 or newer, this is the ftp-proxy version to use.

This applies to OpenBSD 3.9 and newer and equivalents.

The new-style ftp-proxy interacts with your rule set via a set of *anchors*, where the proxy inserts and deletes the rules it constructs to handle your FTP traffic. Just like its predecessor, the ftp-proxy configuration is mainly cut and pasted from the man page.

If you are upgrading to the new ftp-proxy from an earlier version, remove the `ftp-proxy` line from your *inetd.conf* file and either restart `inetd` or disable it altogether if your setup no longer requires a running `inetd`.

Next, enable ftp-proxy by adding the following line to your */etc/rc.conf.local* or */etc/rc.conf*:

```
ftpproxy_flags=""
```

You can start the proxy manually by running `/usr/sbin/ftp-proxy` if you like.

Moving on to the *pf.conf* file, you need two anchor definitions in the NAT section:

```
nat-anchor "ftp-proxy/*"
rdr-anchor "ftp-proxy/*"
```

Both are needed, even if your setup does not use NAT. If you are migrating from a previous ftp-proxy version, your rule set probably contains the appropriate redirection already. If not, add it:

```
rdr pass on $int_if proto tcp from any to any port ftp -> 127.0.0.1 \
        port 8021
```

Coming down to the filtering rules, add an anchor for the proxy to fill in:

```
anchor "ftp-proxy/*"
```

Finally, add a pass rule to let the packets pass from the proxy to the rest of the world:

```
pass out proto tcp from $proxy to any port 21 keep state
```

where *$proxy* expands to the address the proxy daemon is bound to.

This example covers a simple setup with clients who need to contact FTP servers elsewhere. The basic configuration here should work well with most combinations of FTP clients and servers. In practice you may need to compensate for quirks on either side of the fence, so for the finer points of ftp-proxy configuration, do look up the various options the proxy offers.

If you are looking for ways to run an FTP server protected by PF and ftp-proxy, you could look into running a separate ftp-proxy in reverse mode (using the -R option), on a separate port with its own set of redirection and pass rules.

Making Your Network Troubleshooting Friendly

Making your network easy to troubleshoot is a potentially large subject. At most times, the debugging or troubleshooting friendliness of your TCP/IP network depends on how you treat the Internet protocol that was designed specifically with debugging in mind, the Internet Control Message Protocol (ICMP).

ICMP is the protocol for sending and receiving *control messages* between hosts and gateways, mainly to provide feedback to a sender about any unusual or difficult conditions en route to the target host.

There is a lot of ICMP traffic, which usually just happens in the background while you are surfing the Web, reading email, or transferring files. Routers (you are aware that you are building one, right?) use ICMP to negotiate packet sizes and other transmission parameters in a process often referred to as *path MTU discovery*.

You may have heard admins referring to ICMP as either "just evil" or, if their understanding runs a little deeper, "a necessary evil." The reason for this attitude is purely historical. A few years back, it was discovered that the networking stacks of several operating systems contained code that could make a machine crash if it was sent a sufficiently large ICMP request.

One of the companies that was hit hard by this was Microsoft, and you can find a lot of material on the *ping of death* bug by using your favorite search engine. However, this all happened in the second half of the 1990s, and all modern operating systems have thoroughly sanitized their network code since then. At least, that's what we are led to believe. One of the early workarounds was to simply block ICMP ECHO (ping) requests or even all ICMP traffic. Now these rule sets have been around for roughly 10 years, and the people who put them there are still scared. There is most likely little or no reason to worry about destructive ICMP traffic anymore, but in the next sections we will cover how to manage just what ICMP traffic passes to or from your network.

Then, Do We Let It All Through?

The obvious question becomes, if ICMP is such a good and useful thing, should we not let it all through, all the time? The answer is, it depends.

Letting diagnostic traffic pass unconditionally makes debugging easier, of course, but it also makes it relatively easy for others to extract information about your network. That means that a rule like

```
pass inet proto icmp from any to any
```

might not be optimal if you want to cloak the internal workings of your network. In all fairness, it should also be said that you will find some ICMP traffic quite harmlessly riding piggyback on your keep state rules.

The Easy Way Out: The Buck Stops Here

The easiest solution could very well be to let all ICMP traffic from your local net through and let probes from elsewhere stop at your gateway:

```
pass inet proto icmp icmp-type $icmp_types from $localnet to any keep state
pass inet proto icmp icmp-type $icmp_types from any to $ext_if keep state
```

Stopping probes at the gateway might be an attractive option anyway, but let us have a look at a few other options that will show you some of PF's flexibility.

Letting ping Through

The rule set we have developed so far has one clear disadvantage: Common troubleshooting commands such as ping and traceroute will not work. That may not matter too much to your users, and since it was the ping command that scared people into filtering or blocking ICMP traffic in the first place, there are apparently some people who feel we are better off without it. If you are in my perceived target audience, you will be rather fond of having those troubleshooting tools available. And with a few small additions to the rule set, they will be. The ping command uses ICMP, and in order to keep our rule set tidy, we start by defining another macro

```
icmp_types = "echoreq"
```

and a rule that uses the definition

```
pass inet proto icmp all icmp-type $icmp_types keep state
```

You may need more or other types of ICMP packets to go through, and you can then expand $icmp_types to a list of those packet types you want to allow.

Helping traceroute

The command traceroute is another command that is quite useful when your users claim that the Internet isn't working. By default, Unix traceroute uses UDP connections according to a set formula based on destination. The following rule[4] works with the traceroute command on all forms of Unix I've had access to, including GNU/Linux:

```
# allow out the default range for traceroute(8):
# "base+nhops*nqueries-1" (33434+64*3-1)
pass out on $ext_if inet proto udp from any to any port 33433 >< 33626 keep state
```

---

[4] This gives us the first taste of what port ranges look like. They are quite useful in some contexts.

Experience so far indicates that traceroute implementations on other operating systems work roughly the same way. One notable exception is Microsoft Windows. On that platform, the *TRACERT.EXE* program uses ICMP ECHO for this purpose. So if you want to let Windows traceroutes through, you need only the first rule from the previous section, which you used to let ping through. The Unix traceroute program can be instructed to use other protocols as well, and it will behave remarkably like its Microsoft counterpart if you use its -I command-line option. You can check the traceroute man page (or its source code, for that matter) for all the details.

This solution was lifted from an *openbsd-misc* post. I've found that list and the searchable list archives (accessible among other places from *http://marc.info*) to be a very valuable resource whenever you need OpenBSD- or PF-related information.

Path MTU Discovery

The last bit I will remind you about when it comes to troubleshooting is the *path MTU discovery*. Internet protocols are designed to be device independent, and one consequence of device independence is that you cannot always reliably predict what the optimal packet size is for a given connection. The main constraint on your packet size is called the *Maximum Transmission Unit*, or *MTU*, which sets the upper limit on the packet size for an interface. The ifconfig command will show you the MTU for your network interfaces.

Modern TCP/IP implementations expect to be able to determine the right packet size for a connection through a process that simply involves sending packets of varying sizes with the "do not fragment" flag set, expecting an ICMP return packet indicating "type 3, code 4" when the upper limit has been reached. Now, you don't need to dive for the RFCs right away. Type 3 means *destination unreachable*, while code 4 is short for *fragmentation needed, but the "do not fragment" flag is set*. So if your connections to networks, which may have MTUs that differ from your own, seem suboptimal, you could try changing your list of ICMP types slightly to let the destination-unreachable packets through:

```
icmp_types = "{ echoreq, unreach }"
```

As you can see, this means we do not need to change the pass rule itself:

```
pass inet proto icmp all icmp-type $icmp_types keep state
```

Now I'll let you in on a little secret: In almost all cases, these rules are not necessary for purposes of path MTU discovery, but they don't hurt either. However, even though the default PF keep state behavior takes care of most of the ICMP traffic you will need, PF does let you filter on all variations of ICMP types and codes. If you want to delve into more detail, the possible types and codes are documented in the icmp(4) and icmp6(4) man pages. The background information is available in the RFCs.

The main Internet RFCs describing ICMP and some related techniques are RFC 792, RFC 950, RFC 1191, RFC 1256, RFC 2521, and RFC 2765, while ICMP updates for IPv6 are found in RFC 1885, RFC 2463, and RFC 2466. These documents are available in a number of places on the Internet, such as *http://www.ietf.org* and *http://www.faqs.org*, and probably also via your package system.

Tables Make Your Life Easier

By this time you may be thinking that this system for creating rules gets awfully static and rigid. There will, after all, be some kinds of data that are relevant to filtering and redirection at a given time but do not deserve to be put into a configuration file! Quite right, and PF offers mechanisms for handling these situations, as well.

Tables are one such feature, useful as lists of IP addresses that can be manipulated without reloading the entire rule set and also when fast lookups are desirable.

Table names are always enclosed in angle brackets (< and >), like this:

```
table <clients> persist { 192.168.2.0/24, !192.168.2.5 }
```

Here the network 192.168.2.0/24 is part of the table with one exception. The address 192.168.2.5 is excluded using the ! operator (logical NOT). The keyword persist makes sure the table itself will exist even if no rules currently refer to it. It is worth noting that it is also possible to load tables from files where each item is on a separate line, such as the file */etc/clients*

```
192.168.2.0/24
!192.168.2.5
```

which in turn is used to initialize the table in */etc/pf.conf*:

```
table <clients> persist file "/etc/clients"
```

So, for example, you can change one of our earlier rules to read

```
pass inet proto tcp from <clients> to any port $client_out
```

to manage outgoing traffic from your client computers. With this in hand, you can manipulate the table's contents live, such as

```
$ sudo pfctl -t clients -T add 192.168.1/16
```

Note that this changes only the in-memory copy of the table, meaning that the change will not survive a power failure or a reboot unless you arrange to store your changes.

You might opt to maintain the on-disk copy of the table using a cron job that dumps the table content to disk at regular intervals, using a command such as

```
$ sudo pfctl -t clients -T show >/etc/clients
```

Alternatively, you could edit the */etc/clients* file and replace the in-memory table contents with the file data:

```
$sudo pfctl -t clients -T replace -f /etc/clients
```

For operations you will be performing frequently, you will sooner or later end up writing shell scripts for tasks such as inserting or removing items or replacing table contents.

One common example that is extremely easy to implement is enforcing network access restrictions via cron jobs that replace the contents of the tables referenced as from addresses in the pass rules at specific times. In some networks you may even need different access rules for different days of the week. The only real limitations lie in your own needs and your creativity.

We will be returning to some handy uses of tables shortly, including a few programs that interact with tables in useful ways.[5]

---

[5] One program that interacts well with PF tables is the DHCP daemon dhcpd. On OpenBSD, see the dhcpd man page and look at the -A and -L flags.

4

WIRELESS NETWORKS
MADE EASY

It is rather tempting to say that on BSD, and on OpenBSD in particular, there's no need to "make wireless networking simple," because it already is. Getting a wireless network running is not very different from getting a wired one running, but there are some issues that turn up simply because we are dealing with radio waves and not wires. We will take some time to look briefly at some of the issues before moving on to the practical steps involved in creating a usable setup.

Once we have covered the basics of getting a wireless network up and running, we will turn to some of the options for making your wireless network more interesting and harder to break.

A Little IEEE 802.11 Background

Setting up any network interface is, in principle, a two-step process: First, establish a link, and then move on to configuring the interface for TCP/IP traffic.

In the case of wired, Ethernet-type interfaces, establishing the link usually consists of plugging in a cable and seeing the link indicator light up. However, some interfaces require extra steps. Networking over dial-up connections, for example, requires telephony steps, such as dialing a number to get a carrier signal.

In the case of IEEE 802.11–style wireless networks, getting the carrier signal involves quite a few steps at the lowest level. First, you need to select the proper channel in the assigned frequency spectrum. Once you find a signal, you need to set a few link-level network identification parameters. Finally, if the station you want to link to uses some form of link-level encryption, you need to set the right kind and probably negotiate some additional parameters.

Fortunately, on BSD systems all configuration of wireless network devices happens via `ifconfig` commands and options, just as you would set up any other network interface.[1]

Still, since we are introducing wireless networks here, we need to look at the security at various levels in the networking stack from this new perspective.

There are basically three kinds of popular and simple IEEE 802.11 security mechanisms, and we will discuss them briefly in the following sections.

NOTE *For a more complete overview of issues surrounding security in wireless networks see, for example, Professor Kjell Jørgen Hole's articles and slides at his site* (http://www.kjhole.com *and* http://www.kjhole.com/Standards/WiFi/WiFiDownloads.html). *For fresh developments in the Wi-Fi field, the Wi-Fi Net News site at* http://wifinetnews.com/archives/cat_security.html *and "The Unofficial 802.11 Security Web Page" at* http://www.drizzle.com/~aboba/IEEE *come highly recommended.*

MAC Address Filtering

The short version of the story about PF and MAC address filtering is that we don't do it.

A number of consumer-grade, off-the-shelf wireless access points offer MAC address filtering, but contrary to common belief, they don't really add much security. The marketing succeeds largely because most consumers are unaware that it is possible to change the MAC address of essentially any wireless network adapter on the market today.[2]

If you really want to try MAC address filtering, you could look into using the `bridge(4)` facility and the MAC-filtering features offered by `brconfig(8)` on OpenBSD. We will be looking at bridges and some of the more useful ways to use them with packet filtering in the next chapter.

---

[1] On some systems, the older, device-specific programs such as wicontrol and ancontrol are still around, but for the most part they are deprecated and in the process of being replaced with `ifconfig` functionality. On OpenBSD, the consolidation into `ifconfig` has been completed.

[2] A quick man page lookup will tell you that the command to change the MAC address for the interface rum0 is simply `ifconfig rum0 lladdr 00:ba:ad:f0:0d:11`.

WEP

One consequence of using radio waves instead of wires to move data is that it is comparatively easy for outsiders to capture your data in transit. The designers of the 802.11 family of wireless network standards seem to have been aware of this fact, and they came up with a solution, which they went on to market under the name *Wired Equivalent Privacy,* or *WEP.*

Unfortunately, the WEP designers came up with their *wired equivalent* encryption without actually reading up on recent research or consulting active researchers in the field. So, the link-level encryption scheme they recommended is considered a pretty primitive home brew among cryptography professionals. It was no great surprise when WEP encryption was reverse-engineered and cracked within a few months after the first products were released.

Even though you can download free tools to descramble WEP-encoded traffic in a matter of minutes, for a variety of reasons it is still widely supported and used. Essentially all IEEE 802.11 equipment out there has support for at least WEP, and a surprising number of products offer MAC address filtering, too.

You should consider network traffic protected only by WEP to be only marginally more secure than data broadcast in the clear. Then again, the token effort needed to crack into a WEP network may be sufficient to deter lazy and unsophisticated attackers.

WPA

It dawned on the 802.11 designers fairly quickly that their WEP system was not quite what it was cracked up to be, so they came up with a revised and slightly more comprehensive solution called *Wi-Fi Protected Access,* or *WPA.*

WPA looks better than WEP, at least on paper, but the specification is arguably too complicated for widespread implementation. In addition, WPA has also attracted its share of criticism over design issues and bugs. Combined with the familiar issues of access to documentation and hardware, free software support varies. If your project specification includes WPA, look carefully at your operating system and driver documentation.

It goes almost without saying that you will need further security measures, such as SSH or SSL encryption, to maintain any significant level of confidentiality for your data stream.

Picking the Right Hardware for the Task

Picking the right hardware is not necessarily a daunting task. On a BSD system, one simple

```
$ apropos wireless
```

command is all you need to enter to see a listing of all manual pages with the word *wireless* in their subject lines.[3]

Even on a freshly installed system, this will give you a complete list of all wireless network drivers available in the operating system. The next step is to read the driver manual pages and compare the lists of compatible devices with what is available as parts or built into the systems you are considering. Take some time to think through your specific requirements. For testing purposes, low-end `rum` or `ural` USB dongles will work. Later, when you are about to build a more permanent infrastructure, you may want to look into higher-end gear. You may also want to read Appendix B.

Setting Up a Simple Wireless Network

To start building our first wireless network, it makes sense to use the basic gateway configuration from the previous chapter as our starting point. In your network design, it is likely that the wireless network is not directly attached to the Internet at large, but the wireless network will require a gateway of some sort. For that reason, it makes sense to reuse the working gateway setup for this wireless access point with some minor modifications we introduce over the next few paragraphs. After all, it is more convenient than starting a new configuration from scratch.

NOTE   *We are in infrastructure-building mode here, and we will be setting up the access point first. If you prefer to look at the client side first, see "The Client Side" on page 40, and then come back to this page.*

As we mentioned earlier, the first step is to make sure you have a supported card and check that the driver loads and initializes the card properly. The boot-time system messages scroll by on the console, but they also get stored in the file */var/run/dmesg.boot*. You can view the file itself or use the output of the `dmesg` command. With a successfully configured PCI card, you should see something like this:

```
ath0 at pci1 dev 4 function 0 "Atheros AR5212" rev 0x01: irq 11
ath0: AR5212 5.6 phy 4.1 rf5111 1.7 rf2111 2.3, ETSI1W, address 00:0d:88:c8:a7:c4
```

If the interface you want to configure is a hot-pluggable type such as a USB or PCCARD device, you can see the kernel messages by viewing the */var/log/messages* file, for example, by running `tail -f` on the file before you plug in the device.

Next, configure the interface to enable the link, and finally, configure the system for TCP/IP. You can do this from the command line, like so:

```
$ sudo ifconfig ath0 up mediaopt hostap mode 11b chan 11 nwid unwiredbsd nwkey 0x1deadbeef9
```

---

[3] In addition, it is possible to look up man pages on the Web. Check *http://www.openbsd.org* and the other projects' websites; they offer keyword-based man page searches.

This command does several things at once. It configures the ath0 interface, enables the interface with the up parameter, and specifies that the interface is an access point for a wireless network with mediaopt hostap; then it explicitly sets the operating mode to 11b, explicitly sets the channel to 11, and finally, uses the nwid parameter to set the network name to unwiredbsd, with the WEP key (nwkey) set to the hexadecimal string 0x1deadbeef9.

Use ifconfig to check that the command successfully configured the interface:

```
$ ifconfig ath0
ath0: flags=8823<UP,BROADCAST,NOTRAILERS,SIMPLEX,MULTICAST> mtu 1500
        lladdr 00:11:95:ca:e6:59
        groups: wlan
        media: IEEE802.11 autoselect mode 11b hostap
        status: no network
        ieee80211: nwid unwiredbsd chan 11 bssid 00:11:95:ca:e6:59 nwkey <not displayed>
        inet6 fe80::211:95ff:feca:e659%ath0 prefixlen 64 tentative scopeid 0x5
```

Note the contents of the media: and ieee80211: lines. They should match what you entered on the ifconfig command line. With the link part of your wireless network operational, you can go on to the next step and assign an IP address to the interface:

```
sudo ifconfig ath0 10.50.90.1
```

On OpenBSD, you can achieve both by creating a */etc/hostname.ath0* file, roughly like this:

```
up mediaopt hostap mode 11b chan 11 nwid unwiredbsd nwkey 0x1deadbeef9
inet 10.50.90.1
```

and either running /etc/netstart ath0 (you need to do that as root) or waiting patiently for your next boot to complete.

Note that the configuration is divided over two lines. The first line generates an ifconfig command that sets up the interface with the correct parameters for the physical wireless network. The second command, which sets the IP address, is executed only after the first one completes. It is worth noting that since this is our access point, we set the channel explicitly, and we enable a weak WEP encryption by setting the nwkey parameter.

On FreeBSD and NetBSD, you can normally combine all the parameters in one *rc.conf* setting:

```
ifconfig_ath0="mediaopt hostap mode 11b chan 11 nwid unwiredbsd nwkey 0x1deadbeef inet 10.50.90.1"
```

However, on some hardware combinations, setting the link-level options and the IP address at the same time fails. If your one-liner configuration fails, you will need to put the two lines in your */etc/start_if.ath0* and substitute your interface name for *ath0* if required.

NOTE *Be sure to check the most up-to-date ifconfig man page for other options that may be more appropriate for your configuration.*

The Access Point's PF Rule Set

With the interfaces configured, it's time to start configuring the access point as a packet-filtering gateway.

You can start by copying the basic gateway setup from Chapter 3. Enable gatewaying via the appropriate entries in the access point's *sysctl.conf* or *rc.conf* file; then copy across the *pf.conf* file. Depending on the parts of the last chapter that were most useful to you, the *pf.conf* file may look something like this:

```
ext_if = "re0"  # macro for external interface - use tun0 or pppoe0 for PPPoE
int_if = "re1"  # macro for internal interface
localnet = $int_if:network
client_out = "{ ssh, domain, pop3, auth, nntp, http,\
               https, cvspserver, 2628, 5999, 8000, 8080 }"
udp_services = "{ domain, ntp }"
icmp_types = "{ echoreq, unreach }"
# ext_if IP address could be dynamic, hence ($ext_if)
nat on $ext_if from $localnet to any -> ($ext_if)
block all
pass quick inet proto { tcp, udp } from $localnet to any port $udp_services
pass log inet proto icmp all icmp-type $icmp_types
pass inet proto tcp from $localnet to any port $client_out
```

The only change that is strictly necessary for your access point to work is to make the definition of int_if to match the wireless interface. In our example, this means the line should now read

```
int_if = "ath0"  # macro for internal interface
```

More likely than not, you will also want to set up dhcpd to serve addresses and other relevant network information to clients after they have associated with your access point. Setting up dhcpd is fairly straightforward if you read the man pages.

That's all there is to it. This configuration gives you a functional BSD access point, with at least token security (actually more like a *KEEP OUT* sign) via WEP encryption. If you need to support FTP, you can copy the ftp-proxy configuration from the machine you set up in Chapter 3 and make similar changes as for the rest of the rule set.

If Your Access Point Has Three or More Interfaces

If your network design dictates that your access point is also the gateway for a wired local network or even several wireless networks, you need to make some minor changes to your rule set. Instead of just changing the value of the int_if macro, you might want to add another (descriptive) definition for the wireless interface, such as

```
air_if = "ath0"
```

In a wireless gateway configuration, your wireless interfaces are likely to be on separate subnets, so it might be useful for each of them to have its own nat rule as well:

```
nat on $ext_if from $air_if:network to any -> ($ext_if) static-port
```

Depending on your policy, you might also want to adjust your localnet definition or at least include $air_if in your pass rules, where appropriate. And once again, if you need to support FTP, a separate redirection for the wireless network to ftp-proxy may be in order.

Handling IPsec, VPN Solutions

The details of setting up Virtual Private Networks (VPNs) using the built-in IPsec tools, OpenSSH, or other tools are beyond the scope of this chapter. However, with the relatively poor security profile of wireless networks in general, you are likely to want to set up some additional security. A VPN setup may range from useful to essential in your situation.

The options fall roughly into three categories:

SSH

> If your VPN is based on SSH tunnels, the baseline rule set already contains all the filtering you need. Your tunneled traffic will be indistinguishable from other SSH traffic to the packet filter.

IPsec with udp key exchange (IKE/ISAKMP)

> Several IPsec variants depend critically on key exchange via proto udp port 500 and proto {tcp, udp} port 4500 for NAT Traversal (NAT-T). You need to let this traffic through in order to let the flows become established. Some implementations also depend critically on letting ESP protocol traffic (protocol 50) pass between the hosts: pass proto esp from $source to $target.

Filtering on the IPsec encapsulation interface

> With a properly configured IPsec setup, you can set up PF to filter on the encapsulation interface enc0 itself: pass on enc0 proto ipencap from $source to $target keep state (if-bound).

Check Appendix A for references to some useful literature on the subject.

The Client Side

As long as you have all BSD clients, setup is extremely easy. In order to connect to the access point we just configured, your OpenBSD clients would need a *hostname.if* configuration file with

```
up media autoselect mode 11b chan 11 nwid unwiredbsd nwkey 0x1deadbeef9
dhcp
```

Try these out from the command line first, with

```
$ sudo ifconfig ath0 up mode 11b chan 11 nwid unwiredbsd nwkey 0x1deadbeef9
```

followed by

```
$ sudo dhclient ath0
```

The `ifconfig` command should complete without any output, while the `dhclient` command should print a summary of its dialog with the DHCP server:

```
DHCPREQUEST on ath0 to 255.255.255.255 port 67
DHCPREQUEST on ath0 to 255.255.255.255 port 67
DHCPACK from  10.50.90.1
bound to 10.50.90.11 -- renewal in 1800 seconds.
```

Again on FreeBSD, you would need to put those lines in your */etc/start_if.ath0* and substitute your interface name for *ath0* if required.

Guarding Your Wireless Network with authpf

As always, there are other ways to configure the security of your wireless network besides the one we have just seen. What little protection WEP encryption offers, security professionals tend to agree, is barely enough to signal to an attacker that you do not intend to let all and sundry use your network resources.

The configuration we built in "Setting Up a Simple Wireless Network" on page 36 is functional. It will let all reasonably configured wireless clients connect, and that may be a problem in itself, since that configuration does not have any real support built in for letting you decide who uses your network.

As we mentioned earlier, MAC address filtering is not really a solid defense against attackers. Changing the MAC address is just too easy. The OpenBSD developers chose a radically different approach to this problem when they introduced authpf in OpenBSD version 3.1. Instead of tying access to a hardware identifier such as the network card's MAC address, the OpenBSD developers decided that the robust and highly flexible *user* authentication mechanisms already in place were more appropriate for the task. The authpf tool is a user shell that lets the system load PF rules on a per-user basis, effectively deciding which user gets to do what.

To use authpf, you create users with the authpf program as their shell. In order to get network access, the user logs in to the gateway using ssh. Once the user successfully completes ssh authentication, authpf loads the rules you have defined for the user or the relevant class of users.

These rules, which apply to the IP address the user logged in from, stay loaded and in force for as long as the user stays logged in via the ssh connection. Once the ssh session is terminated, the rules are unloaded, and in most scenarios all non-ssh traffic from the user's IP address is denied. With a reasonable setup, only traffic originated by authenticated users will be let through.

It is worth noting that on OpenBSD, authpf is one of the login classes that is offered by default, as you will notice the next time you create a user with the adduser program.

For other systems where the authpf login class is not available by default, you may need to add the following lines to your *login.conf*:

```
authpf:\
        :welcome=/etc/motd.authpf:\
        :shell=/usr/sbin/authpf:\
        :tc=default:
```

The following sections contain a few examples that may or may not fit your situation directly, but I hope they will give you ideas you can use.

A Basic Authenticating Gateway

Setting up an authenticating gateway with authpf involves creating and maintaining a few files besides your basic *pf.conf*. The main addition is *authpf.rules*; the other files are fairly static entities that you will not be spending much time on once they have been created.

Start with creating an empty */etc/authpf/authpf.conf*. It needs to be there for authpf to work, but it doesn't actually need any content, so creating an empty file with touch is appropriate.

The other relevant bits of */etc/pf.conf* follow. First, we create the interface macros:

```
ext_if = "re0"
int_if = "ath0"
```

In addition, authpf requires a table to fill with the IP addresses of authenticated users:

```
table <authpf_users> persist
```

The nat rules, if you need them, could just as easily go in *authpf.rules*, but keeping them in the *pf.conf* file does not hurt in a simple setup like this:

```
nat on $ext_if from $localnet to any -> ($ext_if)
```

Next, we create the authpf anchors, where rules from *authpf.rules* are loaded once the user authenticates:

```
nat-anchor "authpf/*"
rdr-anchor "authpf/*"
binat-anchor "authpf/*"
anchor "authpf/*"
```

That brings us to the end of the required parts of a *pf.conf* for an authpf setup.

For the filtering part, we start with the block all default and then add the pass rules we need. The only thing we really need at this point is to pass ssh on the internal network:

```
pass quick on $int_if inet proto { tcp, udp } to $int_if port ssh
```

From here on out, it really is up to you. Do you want to let your clients have name resolution before they authenticate? If so, put the pass rules for the tcp and udp service domain in your *pf.conf,* too.

For a relatively simple and egalitarian setup, you could include the rest of our baseline rule set, but change the pass rules to allow traffic from the addresses in the <authpf_users> table rather than any address in your local network:

```
pass quick inet proto { tcp, udp } from <authpf_users> to any port $udp_services
pass inet proto tcp from <authpf_users> to any port $client_out
```

For a more differentiated setup, you could put the rest of your rule set in */etc/authpf/authpf.rules* or put per-user rules in customized *authpf.rules* files in each user's directory under */etc/authpf/users/*. If your users normally need some protection, your general */etc/authpf/authpf.rules* could have content like this:

```
client_out = "{ ssh, domain, pop3, auth, nntp, http, https }"
udp_services = "{ domain, ntp }"
pass quick inet proto { tcp, udp } from $user_ip to any port $udp_services
pass inet proto tcp from $user_ip to any port $client_out
```

The macro $user_ip is built into authpf and expands to the IP address the user authenticated from. These rules apply to any user who completes authentication at your gateway.

A nice and relatively easy addition to implement is special-case rules for users with different requirements than your general user population. If an *authpf.rules* file exists in the user's directory under */etc/authpf/users/*, the rules in that file will be loaded for the user.

This means that your naïve Windows user Peter, who only needs to surf the Web and have access to a service that runs on a high port on a specific machine, could get what he needs with a */etc/authpf/users/peter/authpf.rules* file like this:

```
client_out = "{ domain, http, https }"
pass inet from $user_ip to 192.168.103.84 port 9000
pass quick inet proto { tcp, udp } from $user_ip to any port $client_out
```

On the other hand, Peter's colleague Christina runs OpenBSD and generally knows what she's doing, even if she sometimes generates traffic to and from odd ports. You could let her have free rein by putting this in */etc/authpf/users/christina/authpf.rules*:

```
pass from $user_ip os = "OpenBSD" to any
```

This means Christina can do pretty much anything she likes over TCP, as long as she authenticates from her OpenBSD machines.

Wide Open but Actually Shut

In some situations it makes sense to set up your network to be open and unencrypted at the link level, while enforcing some restrictions via authpf. The next example is very similar to Wi-Fi zones you can encounter in airports or other public spaces, in which anyone can associate to the access points and get an IP address, but any attempt at accessing the Web will be redirected to one specific web page until the user has cleared some sort of authentication.[4]

The following *pf.conf* file is again based on our baseline, with two important additions to the basic authpf setup: a macro and a redirection.

```
ext_if = "re0"
int_if = "ath0"
auth_web="192.168.27.20"
dhcp_services = "{ bootps, bootpc }" # DHCP server + client
table <authpf_users> persist
rdr pass on $int_if proto tcp from ! <authpf_users> to any port http ->
$auth_web
nat on $ext_if from $localnet to any -> ($ext_if)
nat-anchor "authpf/*"
rdr-anchor "authpf/*"
binat-anchor "authpf/*"
anchor "authpf/*"
pass quick on $int_if inet proto { tcp, udp } to $int_if port dhcp_services
pass quick inet proto { tcp, udp } from $int_if:network to any port domain
pass quick on $int_if inet proto { tcp, udp } to $int_if port ssh
```

---

[4] Thanks to Vegard Engen for the idea and showing me his configuration, which is preserved here in spirit, if not in every detail.

The auth_web macro and the redirection make sure all web traffic from addresses that are not in the <authpf_users> table leads all nonauthenticated users to a specific address.

At that address you set up a webserver that serves up whatever it is you need. This could be anything from a single page with instructions on who to contact in order to get access to the network, all the way up to a system that accepts credit cards and handles user account creation.

It is worth noting that name resolution will work in this setup, but all surfing attempts will end up at the auth_web address. Once the users clear authentication, you can add general rules or user-specific ones to the *authpf.rules* files as appropriate for your situation.

5

BIGGER OR TRICKIER NETWORKS

In this chapter we'll build on the material from the previous chapters while trying to meet the real-life challenges of larger networks or even smaller ones with relatively demanding applications or users. The sample configurations in this chapter are all based on the assumption that your packet-filtering setups will need to accommodate services you run on your local network. We will mainly be looking at this from a Unix perspective, focusing on SSH, email, and Web services, with some pointers on how to take care of others.

When Others Need Something in Your Network: Filtering Services

Time passes, and needs change. The change could be that your organization and the network grow or that you have decided to take the plunge and move critical points in your corporate infrastructure to BSD and PF.

This chapter is about the things you will want to do when you need to combine packet filtering with services that are accessible outside your local network. How much this complicates your rule sets depends on your network design—and to a certain extent, on the number of routable addresses you have available.

Over the following pages we will deal with the basics of filtering in networks with externally accessible services. We will begin with configurations for official, routable addresses as the baseline and then move on to situations with as few as one routable address and the PF-based workarounds that make the services usable, even under these restrictions.

A Webserver and a Mail Server on the Inside—Routable Addresses

How complicated is your network? How complicated does it need to be?

Let's start with a baseline scenario where the example clients from Chapter 3 get three new neighbors: a mail server, a webserver, and a fileserver. In this scenario we use official, routable addresses, since it makes life a little easier. Using routable addresses has other advantages, too: With routable addresses we can let two of the new machines run the domain name service (DNS) for our *example.com* domain, one as the master, the other as an authoritative slave.[1]

NOTE   *For DNS it always makes sense to have at least one authoritative slave server somewhere outside your own network (in fact, some top-level domains will not let you register a domain unless you have that arrangement). You may also want to arrange for a backup mail server to be hosted elsewhere. Keep these things in mind as you build your network. However, these concerns do not affect how we write the PF rule set much.*

At this stage we keep the physical network layout fairly simple. We put the new servers into the same local network as the clients, possibly in a separate server room, but certainly on the same network segment or switch as the clients. Conceptually, the new network looks something like Figure 5-1.

With the basic parameters for the network in place, we can start setting up a sensible rule set for handling the services we need. Once again we start from the baseline rule set and add a few macros for readability.

The macros we need come rather naturally from the specifications. The ones we need are our webserver (webserver = "192.0.2.227") and the services it offers (webports = "{ http, https }"); the mail server (emailserver = "192.0.2.225") and the services it offers (email = "{ smtp, pop3, imap, imap3, imaps, pop3s }"); and finally, the nameservers (nameservers = "{ 192.0.2.221, 192.0.2.223 }").

We assume that the fileserver does not need to be accessible to the outside world unless we choose to set it up with a service that needs to be visible outside the local network, such as an authoritative slave nameserver for our domain.

---

[1] In fact, the *example.com* network here lives in the 192.0.2.0/24 block, which is set aside in RFC 3330 as reserved for example and documentation use. We use this address range mainly to differentiate from the NAT examples elsewhere in this book, which use addresses in the "private" RFC 1918 address space.

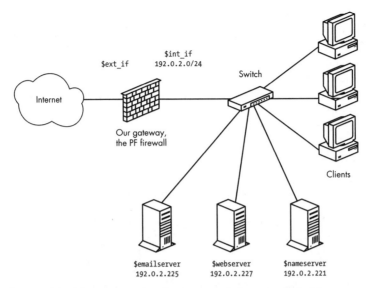

Figure 5-1: A basic network with servers and clients on the inside

With the macros in hand, we add the pass rules. Starting with the web-server, we make it accessible to the world with

```
pass proto tcp from any to $webserver port $webports synproxy state
```

Notice the synproxy state option. When a new connection is created, PF normally lets the communication partners handle the connection setup themselves, simply passing the packets on if they match a pass rule. With synproxy enabled, PF handles the initial connection setup and hands over the connection to the communication partners only when it is properly established. PF acting as an intermediary or proxy for a three-way handshake helps protect against SYN-flood attacks and similar nastiness that could lead to resource exhaustion at the server end. However, SYN proxying is slightly more resource intensive than the default keep state, and it could lead to noticeably increased load on your firewall.

On a similar note, we let the world talk to the mail server:

```
pass proto tcp from any to $emailserver port $email synproxy state
```

It is worth mentioning that this lets clients anywhere have the same access as the ones in your local network, including a few email-retrieval protocols that run without encryption. That's common enough in the real world, but you might want to consider your options if you are setting up a new network.

For the mail server to be useful, it needs to be able to send email to hosts outside the local network, too:

```
pass log proto tcp from $emailserver to any port smtp synproxy state
```

Keeping in mind that the rule set starts with a `block all` rule, this means only the mail server is allowed to initiate SMTP traffic from the local network to the rest of the world. If any of the other hosts on the network need to send email to the outside world or receive email, they need to use the designated mail server. This could be a good way to ensure, for example, that you make it as hard as possible for any spam-sending zombie machines that might turn up in your network to actually deliver their payloads.

Finally, the nameservers need to be accessible to clients outside our network who look up the information about *example.com* and any other domains we answer authoritatively for:

```
pass inet proto { tcp, udp } from any to $nameservers port domain
```

With all services that need to be accessible from the outside world integrated, our rule set ends up looking roughly like this:

```
ext_if = "ep0"  # macro for external interface - use tun0 or pppoe0 for PPPoE
int_if = "ep1"  # macro for internal interface
localnet = $int_if:network
webserver = "192.0.2.227"
webports = "{ http, https }"
emailserver = "192.0.2.225"
email = "{ smtp, pop3, imap, imap3, imaps, pop3s }"
nameservers = "{ 192.0.2.221, 192.0.2.223 }"
client_out = "{ ssh, domain, pop3, auth, nntp, http,\
                https, cvspserver, 2628, 5999, 8000, 8080 }"
udp_services = "{ domain, ntp }"
icmp_types = "{ echoreq, unreach }"
block all
pass quick inet proto { tcp, udp } from $localnet to any port $udp_services
pass log inet proto icmp all icmp-type $icmp_types
pass inet proto tcp from $localnet to any port $client_out
pass inet proto { tcp, udp } from any to $nameservers port domain
pass proto tcp from any to $webserver port $webports synproxy state
pass log proto tcp from any to $emailserver port $email synproxy state
pass log proto tcp from $emailserver to any port smtp synproxy state
```

This is still a fairly simple setup, but unfortunately, it has one potentially troubling security disadvantage. The way this network is designed, the servers that offer services to the world at large are all *in the same local network* as your clients, and you would need to restrict any internal services to only local access. In principle this means that an attacker would only need to compromise one host in your local network to gain access to any resource there, putting the miscreant on equal footing with any user in your local network. Depending on how well each machine and resource are protected from unauthorized access, this could be anything from a minor annoyance to a major headache.

In the next section we look at some options for segregating the services that need to interact with the world at large from the local network.

A Degree of Physical Separation: Introducing the DMZ

In the previous section we showed that it is possible to set up services on your local network and make them selectively available to the outside world through a sensible PF rule set. However, you can get more fine-grained control over access to your internal network, as well as the services you need to make visible to the rest of the world, by introducing a degree of physical separation.

Achieving the physical and logical separation is fairly easy. Move the machines that run the public services to a separate network, attached to a separate interface on the gateway. The net effect is a separate network that is not quite part of your local network but not entirely in the public part of the Internet, either. Conceptually, the segregated network looks like Figure 5-2.

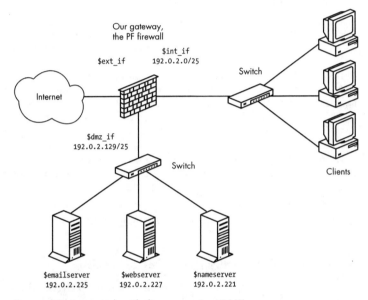

Figure 5-2: A network with the servers in a DMZ

NOTE *You can think of this little network as a zone of relative calm between the territories of hostile factions, and it is no great surprise that a few years back, somebody coined the phrase* De-Militarized Zone, *or* DMZ, *to describe this type of configuration. The term stuck.*

For address allocation, either segment off an appropriately sized chunk of your official address space for the new DMZ network, or move those parts of your network that do not have a specific need to run with publicly accessible and routable addresses into a NATed environment. Either way, you end up with at least one more interface to filter on. As you will see later, it is in fact possible to run a DMZ setup in all-NAT environments too, if you are really short on official addresses.

The adjustments to the rule set itself need not be extensive. If necessary, you can change the configuration for each interface. The basic rule set logic remains, but you may need to adjust the definitions of the macros (`webserver`, `mailserver`, `nameservers`, and possibly others) to reflect your new network layout.

In our example, we could choose to segment off the part of our address range where we have already placed our servers, and if we leave some room for growth, we can set up the new dmz_if on a /25 subnet with an address and netmask of 192.0.2.129/255.255.255.128. With that configuration, you do not really need to touch the rule set at all for the packet filtering to work after setting up a physically segregated DMZ.

Whether you consider this to be due to laziness or excellent long-range planning is debatable; nevertheless, it underlines the importance of having a sensible address-allocation policy in place.

It might be useful to tighten up your rule set by editing your pass rules so the traffic to and from your servers is allowed to pass only on the interfaces that are actually relevant to the services:

```
pass in on $ext_if proto { tcp, udp } from any to $nameservers port domain
pass in on $int_if proto { tcp, udp } from $localnet to $nameservers port domain
pass out on $dmz_if proto { tcp, udp } from any to $nameservers port domain
pass in on $ext_if proto tcp from any to $webserver port $webports
pass in on $int_if proto tcp from $localnet to $webserver port $webports
pass out on $dmz_if proto tcp from any to $webserver port $webports
pass in log on $ext_if proto tcp from any to $mailserver port smtp
pass in log on $int_if proto tcp from $localnet to $mailserver port $email
pass out log on $dmz_if proto tcp from any to $mailserver port smtp
pass in on $dmz_if from $mailserver to any port smtp
pass out log on $ext_if proto tcp from $mailserver to any port smtp
```

You could choose to make the other pass rules that reference your local network interface-specific too, but if you leave them intact, they will continue to work.

Sharing the Load: Redirecting to a Pool of Addresses

Once you have set up services to be accessible to the world at large, one likely scenario is that over time, one or more of your services grows more sophisticated and resource hungry or simply attracts more traffic than you feel comfortable serving from a single server.

There are a number of ways to make several machines share the load of running a service, including various ways to fine-tune the service itself. The particulars of running a webserver are outside the scope of this book. However, for network-level load balancing, PF offers the basic functionality you need by letting you redirect to pools of several addresses, known as *address pools*.

Take the webserver in our example. We already have the macro for the public IP address (webserver = "192.0.2.227"), which in turn is associated with the hostname that your users have bookmarked, possibly *www.example.com*.

When the time comes to share the load, set up the required number of identical, or at least equivalent, servers and then alter your rule set slightly to introduce the redirection. First, add the macro that describes your webserver pool:

```
webpool = "{ 192.0.2.214, 192.0.2.215, 192.0.2.216, 192.0.2.217 }"
```

Then specify the redirection, which means you may choose to retire the original webserver once the switch is done:

```
rdr on $ext_if from any to $webserver port $webports -> $webpool \
    round-robin sticky-address
```

The `round-robin` option means that PF shares the load between the machines in the pool by cycling through the pool of redirection addresses sequentially. The `sticky-address` option makes sure that new connections from a client are always redirected to the same machine behind the redirection as the initial connection.

The sticky address could be essential if the service depends on client-specific or session-specific parameters, which would be lost if the client was redirected to the equivalent service on a different host. In other contexts, where even load distribution is not an absolute requirement, selecting the redirection address at `random` could be appropriate:

```
rdr on $ext_if from any to $webserver port $webports -> $webpool random
```

It is worth noting that even organizations with large pools of official, routable addresses have opted to introduce NAT between their load-balanced server pools and the Internet at large. This technique works equally well in various NAT-based setups, but moving to NAT offers some additional possibilities and challenges.

Getting Load Balancing Right with hoststated

After you have been running a while with load balancing via round-robin redirection, you may notice that the redirection does not automatically adapt to external conditions. One example is if one or more of the hosts in the list of redirection targets goes down. Unless special steps are taken, traffic will be redirected to the IP addresses in the list of possibilities, even if the target host happens to be unreachable or unable to handle the service requests.

Clearly, a monitoring solution is needed, and fortunately, the OpenBSD base system provides one in the host status daemon `hoststated`. `hoststated` interacts with your PF configuration, providing the ability to weed out non-functioning hosts from your pool.

Introducing `hoststated` into your setup, however, may require some minor changes to your rule set. `hoststated` works in terms of *services* and expects to be able to add or subtract hosts' IP addresses to or from PF *tables*. The daemon interacts with your rule set through a special-purpose redirection anchor named `hoststated`. To see how we can make our sample configuration work a little better by using `hoststated`, we'll look back at the load-balancing rule set.

Starting from the top of your *pf.conf,* add the following line to the NAT section:

```
rdr-anchor "hoststated/*"
```

In the load-balancing rule set, we had the following definition for our webserver pool

```
webpool = "{ 192.0.2.214, 192.0.2.215, 192.0.2.216, 192.0.2.217 }"
```

and this redirection

```
rdr on $ext_if from any to $webserver port $webports -> $webpool \
    round-robin sticky-address
```

To make this configuration work with hoststated, we need to change the webpool definition to table form, like this

```
table <webpool> persist { 192.0.2.214, 192.0.2.215, 192.0.2.216, 192.0.2.217 }
```

and change the redirection to use the new <webpool> table:

```
rdr on $ext_if from any to $webserver port $webports -> <webpool> \
    round-robin sticky-address
```

Once the *pf.conf* parts have been taken care of, we turn to hoststated's own *hoststated.conf* configuration file. The syntax in this configuration file is similar enough to *pf.conf* to make it fairly easy to read and understand. First, we add the macro definitions we will be using later:

```
web1="192.0.2.214"
web2="192.0.2.215"
web3="192.0.2.216"
web4="192.0.2.217"
webserver="192.0.2.227"
sorry_server="192.0.2.200"
```

All of these correspond to definitions in our *pf.conf* file, except the last one. (Its use should become apparent in a few moments.) The default checking interval in hoststated is 10 seconds, which means that a host could potentially be down for almost 10 seconds before it is taken offline. Being cautious, we'll set the checking interval to 5 seconds to minimize visible downtime with the following line:

```
interval 5       # check hosts every 5 seconds
```

Now we make a table called webpool that uses the macros to match the table we just made in the PF configuration:

```
table webpool {
        check http "/status.html" code 200
        timeout 300
        real port 80
        host $web1
```

```
        host $web2
        host $web3
        host $web4
}
```

In addition to defining the member hosts, our table also specifies that hoststated should check to see if a host is available by asking it for the file *status.html*, using the protocol HTTP, and expecting the return code to be equal to 200. This is the expected result for a client asking a running webserver for a file it has available.

No big surprises so far, right? hoststated will take care of excluding hosts from the table if they go down. But what happens if all the hosts in the webpool table go down? Fortunately the developers thought of that too and introduced the concept of *backup tables* for services. This is the last part of the definition for the www service, with the table sorry as the backup table:

```
table sorry {
        check icmp
        real port 80
        host $sorry_server
}
service www {
        virtual ip $webserver port 80
        table webpool
        backup table sorry
}
```

The hosts in the sorry table are what take over if the webpool table becomes empty. This means that you need to configure a service that is able to offer a "Sorry, we're down" message in case all the hosts in your web pool fail.

If you want to enable hoststated at startup, add the line

```
hoststated_flags=""     # for normal use: ""
```

to your *rc.conf.local*. However, most of your interaction with hoststated will happen through the hoststatectl administration program. In addition to letting you monitor status, hoststatectl lets you reload the hoststated configuration and selectively disable or enable hosts, tables, and services, and it even lets you view service status interactively, like this:

```
$ sudo hoststatectl show summary
Type      Id    Name               Avlblty Status
service    0    www                        active
table      0    webpool                    active (2 hosts up)
host       3    192.0.2.217        0.00%   down
host       2    192.0.2.216        100.00% up
host       1    192.0.2.215        0.00%   down
host       0    192.0.2.214        100.00% up
table      1    sorry                      active (1 hosts up)
host       4    192.0.2.200        100.00% up
```

Here the web pool is seriously degraded, with only two of four hosts up and running. Fortunately, the backup table is still functioning. Here, all tables are active with at least one host up. For tables that no longer have any members, the Status column changes to empty.

Asking hoststatectl for host information shows the status information in a host-centered format:

```
$ sudo hoststatectl show hosts
Type      Id    Name                   Avlblty  Status
service   0     www                             active
table     0     webpool                         active (2 hosts up)
host      3     192.0.2.217            0.00%    down
                total: 0/6 checks
host      2     192.0.2.216            100.00%  up
                total: 0/6 checks
host      1     192.0.2.215            0.00%    down
                total: 0/6 checks
host      0     192.0.2.214            100.00%  up
                total: 6/6 checks
table     1     sorry                           active (1 hosts up)
host      4     192.0.2.200            100.00%  up
                total: 6/6 checks
```

If you need to take a host out of the pool for maintenance or any time-consuming operations, you can use hoststatectl to disable it with the following command:

```
$ sudo hoststatectl host disable  192.168.103.1
```

In most cases, the operation will display command succeeded to indicate that the operation completed successfully. Once you have done whatever maintenance was needed and put the machine online, you can reenable it as part of hoststated's pool with this command:

```
$ sudo hoststatectl host enable  192.168.103.1
```

Again, you should see the message command succeeded almost immediately to indicate that the operation was successful.

In addition to the basic load balancing we have demonstrated here, hoststated has been extended in recent OpenBSD versions to offer a number of other features that make it attractive in more complex settings. It can now handle Layer 7 proxying or relaying functions for HTTP and HTTPS. This includes protocol handling with header append and rewrite, URL path append and rewrite, and even session and cookie handling.

The protocol handling needs to be tailored to your application. The following is a simple HTTPS relay for load balancing the encrypted web traffic from clients to the webservers.

```
protocol httpssl {
        protocol http
                header append "$REMOTE_ADDR" to "X-Forwarded-For"
                header append "$SERVER_ADDR:$SERVER_PORT" to "X-Forwarded-By"
                header change "Keep-Alive" to "$TIMEOUT"
                url hash "sessid"
                cookie hash "sessid"
                path filter "*command=*" from "/cgi-bin/index.cgi"

                ssl { sslv2, ciphers "MEDIUM:HIGH" }
                tcp { nodelay, sack, socket buffer 65536, backlog 128 }

}
```

The protocol handler definition shown here demonstrates a range of simple operations on the HTTP headers and sets both SSL parameters and specific TCP parameters to optimize connection handling. The header options operate on the protocol headers, inserting the values of the variables by either appending to existing headers (append) or changing the content to a new value (change). The url and cookie hashes are used by the load balancer to select which host in the target pool the request is forwarded to. The path filter specifies that any get request, including the first quoted string as a substring of the second, is to be dropped. The ssl options specify that only SSL version 2 ciphers are accepted, with key lengths in the medium-to-high range, or, in other words, 128 bits or more.[2] Finally, the tcp options specify that the ToS flag should be set to nodelay, specify that the selective acknowl-edgment method (RFC 2018) is to be used, and set the socket buffer size and the maximum allowed number of pending connections the load balancer keeps track of.

The relay definition using the protocol handler follows a pattern that should be familiar from the service definition for the www service we defined earlier:

```
relay wwwssl {
        # Run as a SSL accelerator
        listen on $webserver port 443 ssl
        protocol httpssl
        table webhosts loadbalance
}
```

However, it is likely that your SSL-enabled web applications will benefit from a slightly different set of parameters.

Finally, for CARP-based failover of the hosts running hoststated for your network (see "Redundancy and Failover: CARP and pfsync" on page 97) hoststated can be configured to support CARP interaction via setting the CARP demotion counter for the specified interface groups or groups at shutdown or startup. Like all parts of the OpenBSD system, hoststated comes with

---

[2] See the OpenSSL man page for further explanation of cipher-related options.

informative documentation in the form of man pages. For the angles and options we have not covered here (there are a few), I recommend that you dive into the man pages for hoststated, *hoststated.conf*, and hoststatectl and start experimenting to find just the configuration you need.

A Webserver and a Mail Server on the Inside—The NAT Version

Let's backtrack a little and start over with the baseline scenario in which the example clients from Chapter 3 get three new neighbors: a mail server, a webserver, and a fileserver. This time around, externally visible addresses are either not available or too expensive, and running several other services on a machine that is primarily a firewall is not a desirable option.

This means we are back to the situation where we do our NAT at the gateway. Fortunately, the redirection mechanisms in PF make it relatively easy to keep servers on the inside of a NATing gateway. The network specifications are the same as for the *example.com* setup we just worked through: We need to run a webserver that serves up data in clear text (http) and encrypted (https), and in addition we want a mail server that sends and receives email while letting clients inside and outside the local network use a number of well-known submission and retrieval protocols:

```
webserver = "192.168.2.7"
webports = "{ http, https }"
emailserver = "192.168.2.5"
email = "{ smtp, pop3, imap, imap3, imaps, pop3s }"

rdr on $ext_if proto tcp from any to $ext_if port $webports -> $webserver
rdr on $ext_if proto tcp from any to $ext_if port $email -> $emailserver

pass proto tcp from any to $webserver port $webports synproxy state
pass proto tcp from any to $emailserver port $email synproxy state
pass proto tcp from $emailserver to any port smtp synproxy state
```

Once again, we use the flag synproxy in the new rules. This means that PF will handle the connection setup (three-way handshake) on behalf of your server or client before handing the connection over to the applications running at either end. This provides a certain amount of protection against SYN-based attacks, as we saw earlier.

DMZ with NAT

With an all-NAT setup, the pool of available addresses to allocate for a DMZ is likely to be larger than in our previous example in "A Degree of Physical Separation: Introducing the DMZ" on page 49, but the same principles apply. When you move the servers off to a physically separate network, you will need to check that your rule set's macro definitions are sane, and adjust the values if necessary.

Just as in the routable addresses case, it might be useful to tighten up your rule set by editing your pass rules so the traffic to and from your servers is allowed to pass only on the interfaces that are actually relevant to the services:

```
pass in on $ext_if proto { tcp, udp } from any to $nameservers port domain
pass in on $int_if proto { tcp, udp } from $localnet to $nameservers port domain
pass out on $dmz_if proto { tcp, udp } from any to $nameservers port domain
pass in on $ext_if proto tcp from any to $webserver port $webports
pass in on $int_if proto tcp from $localnet to $webserver port $webports
pass out on $dmz_if proto tcp from any to $webserver port $webports
pass in log on $ext_if proto tcp from any to $mailserver port smtp
pass in log on $int_if proto tcp from $localnet to $mailserver port $email
pass out log on $dmz_if proto tcp from any to $mailserver port smtp
pass in on $dmz_if from $mailserver to any port smtp
pass out log on $ext_if proto tcp from $mailserver to any port smtp
```

If it makes sense in your context to make other specific pass rules that reference your local network interface, you could choose to do so, but if you leave them intact, they will continue to work.

Redirection for Load Balancing

The redirection-based load-balancing rules from "Sharing the Load: Redirecting to a Pool of Addresses" on page 50 work equally well in a NAT regime where the public address is the gateway's external interface and the redirection addresses are in a private range.

The main difference between the routable address case and the NAT version is that after you have added the webpool definition

```
webpool = "{ 192.168.2.7, 192.168.2.8, 192.168.2.9, 192.168.2.10 }"
```

you edit the existing redirection, which then becomes

```
rdr on $ext_if from any to $webserver port $webports -> $webpool \
    round-robin sticky-address
```

From that point on, your NATed DMZ behaves much like the one with official, routable addresses.

Back to the Single NATed Network

It may surprise you to hear that there are cases where setting up a small network is in fact more difficult than working with a large one.

Going back to the situation where the servers are on the same physical network as the clients, the basic NATed configuration from "A Webserver and a Mail Server on the Inside—The NAT Version" on page 56 works very well, up to a point. In fact, everything works brilliantly as long as all you are interested in is getting traffic from hosts outside your local net to reach your servers.

To save you from paging back and forth, here is the basic configuration:

```
webserver = "192.168.2.7"
webports = "{ http, https }"
emailserver = "192.168.2.5"
email = "{ smtp, pop3, imap, imap3, imaps, pop3s }"

nat on $ext_if from $localnet to any -> ($ext_if)

rdr on $ext_if proto tcp from any to $ext_if port $webports -> $webserver
rdr on $ext_if proto tcp from any to $ext_if port $email -> $emailserver

pass proto tcp from any to $webserver port $webports synproxy state
pass proto tcp from any to $emailserver port $email synproxy state
pass proto tcp from $emailserver to any port smtp synproxy state
```

If you try to reach the services on the official address from hosts in your own network, you will soon see that the requests for the redirected services from machines in your local network most likely never reach the external interface. This is because all the redirection and translation happens on the external interface.

The gateway receives the packets from your local net on the internal interface, with the destination address set to the external interface's address. The gateway recognizes the address as one of its own and tries to handle the request as if it was directed at a local service. Consequently, the redirections do not quite work from the inside.

Fortunately, several workarounds for this particular problem are possible. The problem is common enough that the *PF User Guide* lists four different solutions to it,[3] including moving your servers to a DMZ, as we described earlier. Since this is a PF book, we will concentrate on a PF-based solution, which consists of treating the local net as a special case for our redirection and nat rules.

We need to intercept the network packets originating in the local network and handle those connections correctly, making sure that any return traffic is directed to the communication partner who actually originated the connection.

This means that for the redirections to work as expected from the local network, we need to add special-case redirection rules that mirror the ones designed to handle requests from the outside:

```
rdr on $int_if proto tcp from $localnet to $ext_if port $webports -> $webserver
rdr on $int_if proto tcp from $localnet to $ext_if port $email -> $emailserver
no nat on $int_if proto tcp from $int_if to $localnet
nat on $int_if proto tcp from $localnet to $webserver port $webports -> $int_if
nat on $int_if proto tcp from $localnet to $emailserver port $email -> $int_if
```

---

[3] See "Redirection and Reflection" in the *PF User Guide* (*http://www.openbsd.org/faq/pf/ rdr.html#reflect*).

This way, we twist the redirections and the address translation logic to do what we need, and we do not need to touch the pass rules at all. I've had the good fortune to witness, via email or IRC, the reactions of several network admins at the point when the truth about this five-line reconfiguration sank in.

Filtering on Interface Groups

Your network could have several subnets that may never need to interact with your local network except for some common services such as email, Web, file, and print. How you handle the traffic from and to such subnets depends on how your network is designed. One useful approach is to treat each less-privileged network as a separate local network attached to its own separate interface on a common filtering gateway, and then give it a rule set that allows only the desired direct interaction, with the neighboring networks attached to the main gateway.

On the gateway itself, it can be useful to group logically similar interfaces into *interface groups* and apply filtering rules to the groups, rather than the individual interfaces. Interface groups, as implemented via the ifconfig group option, originally appeared in OpenBSD 3.6 and have been adopted in FreeBSD 7.0 onward.

All configured network interfaces can be configured to belong to one or more groups. Some interfaces automatically belong to one of the default groups. For example, all IEEE 802.11 wireless network interfaces belong to the wlan group, while interfaces associated with the default routes belong to the egress group. Fortunately. an interface can be a member of several groups, and you can add interfaces to interface groups via the appropriate ifconfig command, such as

```
# ifconfig sis2 group untrusted
```

(or the equivalent in the *hostname.sis2* file on OpenBSD, or the ifconfig_sis2= line in the *rc.conf* file on FreeBSD 7.0 or later).

Where it makes sense, you can then treat the interface group in much the same way you would handle a single interface in filtering rules:

```
pass in on untrusted to any port $webports
pass out on egress to any port $webports
```

It is worth noting that filtering on interface groups makes it possible to write essentially hardware-independent rule sets. As long as your *hostname.if* files or ifconfig_if= lines put the interfaces in the correct groups, rule sets that consistently filter on interface groups will be fully portable between machines that may or may not have identical hardware configurations.

The Power of Tags

In some networks, the decision of where a packet should be allowed to pass cannot be made merely on the basis of simple criteria like subnet and service. The fine-grained control the site's policy demands could make the rule set complicated and potentially hard to maintain.

Fortunately, PF offers yet another mechanism for classification and filtering in the form of packet tagging. The useful way to implement packet tagging is to tag incoming packets that match a specific pass rule, and then let the packets pass elsewhere based on which identifiers each packet is tagged with.

One example could be the wireless access points we set up in Chapter 4, which we could reasonably expect to inject traffic into the local network with an apparent source address equal to the access point's $ext_if address.

In that scenario, a possibly useful addition to the rule set of a gateway with several of these access points could be

```
wifi = "{ 10.0.0.115, 10.0.0.125, 10.0.0.135, 10.0.0.145 }"
pass in on $int_if from $wifi to $wifi_allowed port $wifi_ports tag wifigood
pass out on $ext_if tagged wifigood
```

given, of course, definitions of the $wifi_allowed and $wifi_ports macros to fit the site's requirements.

As rule set complexity grows in response to changing needs in your networks, it is worth considering the use of tag and tagged in your pass rules to make your rule set readable and easier to maintain. It is worth noting that tags are *sticky*. Once a packet has been tagged by a matching rule, it can potentially be tagged by all other matching rules too, not just the last one. You could, for example, set several tags on incoming traffic via a set of pass rules, supplemented by a set of pass rules that determine where packets pass out based on the tags set on the incoming traffic.[4]

---

[4] In OpenBSD 4.2, ftp-proxy (see "FTP Through NAT: ftp-proxy" on page 25) acquired the ability to tag packets, making it easier to integrate in complex configurations. See the ftp-proxy man page for details.

The Bridging Firewall

An Ethernet *bridge* consists of two or more interfaces that are configured to forward Ethernet frames transparently and are not directly visible to the upper layers, such as the TCP/IP stack. In a filtering context, the bridge configuration is often considered attractive because it means that the filtering can be performed on a machine that does not have any IP addresses of its own. If the machine in question runs OpenBSD or a similarly capable operating system, it is still able to filter and redirect traffic.

The main perceived advantage of such a setup is that attacking the firewall itself is more difficult. The disadvantage is that all admin tasks must be performed at the firewall's console, unless you configure a network interface that is accessible via a secured network of some kind or even a serial console.

It also follows naturally that bridges with no IP address configured cannot be set as the gateway for a network and cannot run any services on the bridged interfaces. Rather, you can think of a bridge as an intelligent bulge on the network cable, which is able to filter and redirect.

A few general caveats apply to using firewalls implemented as bridges:

- The interfaces are placed in promiscuous mode, which means that they can receive any packet on the network.
- Bridges operate on the Ethernet level and, by default, forward all types of packets, not just TCP/IP.
- The lack of IP addresses on the interfaces makes some of the more effective redundancy features, such as carp, unavailable.

The exact method for configuring bridges differs in some details among the operating systems. The following examples are very basic and do not cover all possible wrinkles, but they should be enough to get you started.

Basic Bridge Setup on OpenBSD

The OpenBSD *GENERIC* kernel contains all the necessary code to configure bridges and filter on them. Unless you have compiled a custom kernel without the bridge code, the setup is quite straightforward.

To create a bridge with two interfaces on the command line, first create the bridge device. The first device of a kind is conventionally given the sequence number 0, so we create the bridge0 device with the following command:

```
$ sudo ifconfig bridge0 create
```

Before the next brconfig command, use ifconfig to check that the prospective member interfaces (in our case ep0 and ep1) are up but have not been assigned IP addresses.

Then configure the bridge by entering the command

```
$ sudo brconfig bridge0 add ep0 add ep1 blocknonip ep0 blocknonip ep1 up
```

The OpenBSD `brconfig` command contains a fair bit of filtering code itself, and in this example we chose the `blocknonip` option for each interface to block all non-IP traffic.

NOTE *The OpenBSD `brconfig` command offers its own set of filtering options in addition to other configuration options. The `bridge(4)` and `brconfig(8)` man pages offer further information. It is worth noting that since it operates on the Ethernet level, `brconfig` is able to filter on MAC addresses. `brconfig` is also able to tag packets for further processing in your PF rule set via the `tagged` keyword.*

To make the configuration permanent, create or edit */etc/hostname.ep0* and finally, enter the following line:

```
up
```

For the other interface, you need */etc/hostname.ep1* to contain

```
up
```

and finally, enter the bridge setup in */etc/bridgename.bridge0*:

```
add ep0 add ep1 blocknonip ep0 blocknonip ep1 up
```

This means your bridge is up and you can move on to creating the PF filter rules.

Basic Bridge Setup on FreeBSD

For FreeBSD, the procedure is a little more involved. To be able to use bridging, your running kernel needs to include or be able to load the `if_bridge` module. The default kernel configurations build this module, so under ordinary circumstances, you can go directly to creating the interface.

If you want to compile the bridge device into the kernel, add the line

```
device if_bridge
```

in the kernel configuration file. It is also possible to load the device at boot time by putting the line

```
if_bridge_load="YES"
```

in the */etc/loader.conf* file.

Create the bridge device by issuing the following command:

```
$ sudo ifconfig bridge0 create
```

Creating the bridge0 interface also creates a set of bridge-related sysctls:

```
$ sudo sysctl net.link.bridge
net.link.bridge.ipfw: 0
net.link.bridge.pfil_member: 1
net.link.bridge.pfil_bridge: 1
net.link.bridge.ipfw_arp: 0
net.link.bridge.pfil_onlyip: 1
```

It is worth checking that these sysctl values are available. If they are, it is confirmation that the bridge has been enabled. If they are not, you need to go back and see what went wrong and why. However, these values apply to filtering on the bridge interface itself, so we do not need to touch these values, since IP-level filtering on the member interfaces (the ends of the pipe) is enabled by default.

Before the next ifconfig command, check that the prospective member interfaces (in our case ep0 and ep1) are up but have not been assigned IP addresses.

Then configure the bridge by entering the command

```
$ sudo ifconfig bridge0 addm ep0 addm ep1 up
```

To make the configuration permanent, add the following lines to /etc/rc.conf:

```
ifconfig_ep0="up"
ifconfig_ep1="up"
cloned_interfaces="bridge0"
ifconfig_bridge0="addm ep0 addm ep1 up"
```

This means your bridge is up and you can move on to creating the PF filter rules. See the if_bridge(4) man page for further FreeBSD-specific bridge information.

Basic Bridge Setup on NetBSD

On NetBSD, the default kernel configuration does not have the filtering bridge support compiled in. You need to compile a custom kernel with the option

```
options         BRIDGE_IPF      # bridge uses IP/IPv6 pfil hooks too
```

added to the kernel configuration file. Once you have the new kernel with the bridge code in place, the setup is quite straightforward.

To create a bridge with two interfaces on the command line, first create the bridge0 device:

```
$ sudo ifconfig bridge0 create
```

Before the next `brconfig` command, use `ifconfig` to check that the prospective member interfaces (in our case ep0 and ep1) are up but have not been assigned IP addresses.

Then configure the bridge by entering the command

```
$ sudo brconfig bridge0 add ep0 add ep1 up
```

Next, enable the filtering on the `bridge0` device:

```
$ sudo brconfig bridge0 ipf
```

To make the configuration permanent, create or edit */etc/ifconfig.ep0* and enter the following line:

```
up
```

For the other interface, you need */etc/ifconfig.ep1* to contain

```
up
```

and finally, enter the bridge setup in */etc/ifconfig.bridge0*:

```
create
!add ep0 add ep1 up
```

This means your bridge is up and you can move on to creating the PF filter rules.[5]

The Bridge Rule Set

Here is the *pf.conf* for a bulge-in-the-wire version of the baseline rule set we started with in this chapter. The network again changes slightly, to look like Figure 5-3.

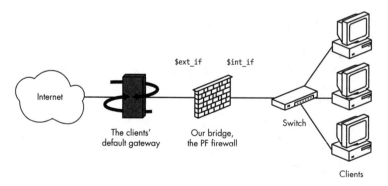

Figure 5-3: A network with a bridge firewall

---

[5] For further information, see the PF on NetBSD documentation at *http://www.netbsd.org/ Documentation/network/pf.html*.

The machines in the local net share a common default gateway, which is not the bridge but could be placed conceptually on either the inside or the outside of the bridge.

```
ext_if = ep0
int_if  = ep1
localnet= "192.0.2.0/24"
webserver = "192.0.2.227"
webports = "{ http, https }"
emailserver = "192.0.2.225"
email = "{ smtp, pop3, imap, imap3, imaps, pop3s }"
nameservers = "{ 192.0.2.221, 192.0.2.223 }"
client_out = "{ ssh, domain, pop3, auth, nntp, http, https, cvspserver, 2628, 5999, 8000, 8080 }"
udp_services = "{ domain, ntp }"
icmp_types = "{ echoreq, unreach }"
set skip on $int_if
block all
pass quick on $ext_if inet proto { tcp, udp } from $localnet to any port $udp_services
pass log on $ext_if inet proto icmp all icmp-type $icmp_types
pass on $ext_if inet proto tcp from $localnet to any port $client_out
pass on $ext_if inet proto { tcp, udp } from any to $nameservers port domain
pass on $ext_if proto tcp from any to $webserver port $webports synproxy state
pass log on $ext_if proto tcp from any to $emailserver port $email synproxy state
pass log on $ext_if proto tcp from $emailserver to any port smtp synproxy state
```

Significantly more complicated setups are possible. Remember, though, that while redirections will work, you will not be able to run services on any of the IP address–less interfaces.

Handling Nonroutable Addresses from Elsewhere

Even with a properly configured gateway to handle filtering and potentially network address translation for your own network, you may find yourself in the unenviable position of having to compensate for other people's misconfigurations.

One depressingly common class of misconfigurations is the kind that lets traffic with nonroutable addresses out to the Internet. Traffic from nonroutable addresses has also played a part in several Denial of Service (DoS) attack techniques, so it may be worth considering explicitly blocking traffic from nonroutable addresses from entering your network.

One possible solution is outlined below, which for good measure also blocks any attempt to initiate contact to nonroutable addresses through the gateway's external interface:

```
martians = "{ 127.0.0.0/8, 192.168.0.0/16, 172.16.0.0/12, \
              10.0.0.0/8, 169.254.0.0/16, 192.0.2.0/24, \
              0.0.0.0/8, 240.0.0.0/4 }"

block in quick on $ext_if from $martians to any
block out quick on $ext_if from any to $martians
```

Here, the martians macro denotes the RFC 1918 addresses and a few other ranges that are mandated by various RFCs not to be in circulation on the open Internet. Traffic to and from such addresses is quietly dropped on the gateway's external interface.

The specific details of how to implement this kind of protection will vary according to your specific network configuration, among other things. Your network design could, for example, dictate that you include or exclude other address ranges than these.

NOTE   *It is worth noting that the martians macro could easily be implemented as a table instead.*

6

TURNING THE TABLES FOR PROACTIVE DEFENSE

In the previous chapter we spent consider-
able time and energy to make sure the
services we want to offer are available even
when we have strict packet filtering in place.
Now that you have a working setup, you will soon
notice that some services tend to attract a little more
unwanted attention than others.

In this chapter, we'll look into how we can use built-in PF features such
as tables and state-tracking options, sometimes in tandem with userspace
programs, to head off the unwanted attention and build a more functional
network.

Here's the scenario: We have set up a network with packet filtering to
match the site's needs, and as part of the package for a functional network,
we have some services running that need to be accessible to users from
elsewhere. Making services available unfortunately means that there is a risk
that somebody, somewhere will want to exploit the opening your service offers
for some sort of mischief.

There are two services you are almost certain to have on your network: remote login via the Secure Shell protocol (ssh) and SMTP email, both tempting targets for the miscreants out there. In the following section, "Turning Away the Brutes," we look at some ways to make it harder to gain unauthorized access via ssh before turning to some of the more effective ways to deny spammers the pleasures of your servers and users in "Giving Spammers a Hard Time with spamd" on page 71.

Turning Away the Brutes

The Secure Shell service, commonly referred to as SSH, is a fairly crucial service for Unix administrators. It's frequently the main interface to a machine, and the fact that it's often enabled on *powerful* systems has made the service a favorite target of script kiddie attacks.

If you run a Secure Shell login service on any machine, I'm sure you've seen things like this in your authentication logs:

```
Sep 26 03:12:34 skapet sshd[25771]: Failed password for root from 200.72.41.31 port 40992 ssh2
Sep 26 03:12:34 skapet sshd[5279]: Failed password for root from 200.72.41.31 port 40992 ssh2
Sep 26 03:12:35 skapet sshd[5279]: Received disconnect from 200.72.41.31: 11: Bye Bye
Sep 26 03:12:44 skapet sshd[29635]: Invalid user admin from 200.72.41.31
Sep 26 03:12:44 skapet sshd[24703]: input_userauth_request: invalid user admin
Sep 26 03:12:44 skapet sshd[24703]: Failed password for invalid user admin from 200.72.41.31
port 41484 ssh2
Sep 26 03:12:44 skapet sshd[29635]: Failed password for invalid user admin from 200.72.41.31
port 41484 ssh2
Sep 26 03:12:45 skapet sshd[24703]: Connection closed by 200.72.41.31
Sep 26 03:13:10 skapet sshd[11459]: Failed password for root from 200.72.41.31 port 43344 ssh2
Sep 26 03:13:10 skapet sshd[7635]: Failed password for root from 200.72.41.31 port 43344 ssh2
Sep 26 03:13:10 skapet sshd[11459]: Received disconnect from 200.72.41.31: 11: Bye Bye
Sep 26 03:13:15 skapet sshd[31357]: Invalid user admin from 200.72.41.31
Sep 26 03:13:15 skapet sshd[10543]: input_userauth_request: invalid user admin
Sep 26 03:13:15 skapet sshd[10543]: Failed password for invalid user admin from 200.72.41.31
port 43811 ssh2
Sep 26 03:13:15 skapet sshd[31357]: Failed password for invalid user admin from 200.72.41.31
port 43811 ssh2
Sep 26 03:13:15 skapet sshd[10543]: Received disconnect from 200.72.41.31: 11: Bye Bye
Sep 26 03:13:25 skapet sshd[6526]: Connection closed by 200.72.41.31
```

It gets repetitive after that, but this is what a brute force attack looks like. Somebody, or more likely a cracked computer somewhere, is trying by brute force to find a username and password that will allow a user to complete a logon and give the attacker access to your system.

The simplest response would be to write a *pf.conf* rule that blocks all access. This leads to another class of problems, though, including how to let people with legitimate business on your system access it anyway. Setting up your sshd to accept only key-based authentication would help too, but most likely it would not stop the kiddies from trying the same thing over and over. You might consider moving the service to some other port, but then again, anyone who is flooding you on port 22 now would probably be able to scan your ports all the way to port 22222 for a repeat performance.

Since OpenBSD 3.7 (or FreeBSD 6.0), PF has offered a slightly more elegant solution. You can write your pass rules so they maintain certain limits on what connecting hosts can do.

For good measure, you can banish violators to a table of addresses for which you deny some or all access. You can even choose to drop all existing connections from machines that overreach your limits, if you like. Here's how it's done.

First, set up the table by adding the following line to your tables section:

```
table <bruteforce> persist
```

Then, somewhere fairly early in your rule set, set up the rule to block traffic from the brute forcers, as shown here:

```
block quick from <bruteforce>
```

And finally, add your pass rule like this:

```
pass inet proto tcp from any to $localnet port $tcp_services \
    keep state (max-src-conn 100, max-src-conn-rate 15/5, \
        overload <bruteforce> flush global)
```

This is rather similar to what we've seen before, isn't it? In fact, the first part is identical to the rule we constructed earlier. What you should pay close attention to is the part in parentheses, called *state-tracking options*. These will ease your network load even further.

max-src-conn is the number of simultaneous connections you allow from one host. In this example, I've set it to 100. However, in your setup you may want a slightly higher or lower value, depending on the traffic patterns on your network.

max-src-conn-rate is the rate of new connections allowed from any single host, here 15 connections per 5 seconds. Again, you are the one to judge what suits your setup.

overload <bruteforce> means that any host that exceeds these limits has its address added to the table <bruteforce>. Our rule set blocks all traffic from addresses in the <bruteforce> table.

WARNING   *It is important to note that once a host has gone over any one of these limits and is put in the overload table, the rule no longer matches traffic from that host. You need to make sure that overloaders are handled, if only by a default block rule or something similar.*

flush global says that when a host reaches the limit, that host's connections will be terminated (flushed). The global part says that for good measure, the flush applies to connections that match other pass rules too.

The effect is dramatic. My brute forcers more often than not end up with Fatal: timeout before authentication messages, which is exactly what we want.

Once again, please keep in mind that this example rule is intended mainly as an illustration. It is not unlikely that your network's needs are better served by different rules or combinations of rules.

Setting the number of simultaneous connections or the rate of connections too low may lead to locking out legitimate traffic. One such scenario with a clear risk of self-inflicted DoS is when the configuration includes a large number of hosts behind a common NATing gateway, and the users on the NATed hosts have legitimate business needs that require them to contact services on the other side of a gateway with strict overload rules.

If, for example, you want to allow a generous number of connections in general but would like to be a little more tight-fisted when it comes to ssh, you could supplement the aforementioned rule with something like the one below, early on in your rule set:

```
pass quick proto { tcp, udp } from any to any port ssh \
    keep state (max-src-conn 15, max-src-conn-rate 5/3, \
        overload <bruteforce> flush global)
```

You should be able to find the set of parameters that is just right for your situation by reading the relevant man pages and the *PF User Guide* (*http://www .openbsd.org/faq/pf*)—and perhaps by doing a bit of experimentation.

You May Not Need to Block All of Your Overloaders

It is probably worth making two points here: The overload mechanism is a general technique that does not have to apply exclusively to the ssh service, and blocking all traffic from offenders is not always desired.

You could, for example, use an overload rule to protect an email service or a web service. Or you could use the overload table in a rule to assign offenders to a queue with a minimal bandwidth allocation (see "Directing Traffic with ALTQ" on page 87). It's also useful, in web cases, for redirecting any and all http requests to a specific web page only (much like in the authpf example in "Wide Open but Actually Shut" on page 43).

Tidying Your Tables with pfctl

At this point, we have tables that will be filled by our overload rules, and since we expect our gateways to have months of uptime, the tables will grow incrementally and take up more memory as time goes by.

At some point, you will probably also find that an IP address you blocked last week because of a brute-force attack was in fact a dynamically assigned one, which is now assigned to a different ISP customer who has a legitimate reason to try communicating with hosts in your network.

Situations like these create the need for a way to remove table entries that are no longer needed. In OpenBSD 4.1, pfctl acquired the ability to *expire* table entries based on the time since their statistics were last reset.

In almost all circumstances, this is equal to the time since the table entry was added. The keyword was, predictably, expire, and the table entry's age was specified in seconds.

For example, the command shown here:

```
# pfctl -t bruteforce -T expire 86400
```

will remove <bruteforce> table entries that had their statistics reset more than 86,400 seconds, or 24 hours, ago. You might want to set up crontab entries to run table expiry at regular intervals, such as every hour, once a day, or several times each day.

The Forerunner: expiretable

Before pfctl acquired the ability to expire table entries, table expiry was more likely than not handled by the special-purpose utility expiretable, written by Henrik Gustafsson. This program performs essentially the same function as pfctl's -T expire feature and is mainly useful for PF implementations based on OpenBSD 4.0 or earlier.

You could let expiretable run as a daemon that removes <bruteforce> table entries older than 24 hours by adding an entry containing the following to your */etc/rc.local* file:

```
/usr/local/sbin/expiretable -v -d -t 24h bruteforce
```

expiretable was quickly added to the ports tree on FreeBSD and OpenBSD, as *security/expiretable* and *sysutils/expiretable*, respectively.

If expiretable is not available via your package system, you can download it from Henrik's site at *http://expiretable.fnord.se*.

Giving Spammers a Hard Time with spamd

One other service that needs some special attention is email. Email is one of the older Internet services and one we would not like to do without. In the form of SMTP and a host of retrieval protocols, email is one of the basic services on any TCP/IP network. So basic, in fact, that it's extremely hard to even imagine what the Internet would be without it.

By the early years of the present century, the commercialized Internet had seen the rise of spam as a problem that threatened to make SMTP email less useful. Various content-filtering solutions were devised, and while a number of the open-source ones ran well on the BSDs, the OpenBSD team set to work on its own spam-fighting solution, dubbed spamd, in early 2003. The first version of spamd was introduced as part of OpenBSD 3.3, which was released on May 1, 2003.

NOTE *In addition to the OpenBSD spam-deferral daemon, the content-filtering based anti-spam package SpamAssassin (http://spamassassin.apache.org) also features a program called spamd. The two programs are both designed to help fight spam, but they represent very different approaches to the underlying problem and do not inter-operate directly. However, when both programs are correctly configured and running in your network, they can complement each other well. The two programs are not related in any way, and care has been taken to make sure their files are installed in separate locations in the filesystem; if there is a need, it is possible to have both spamd programs installed on the same system.*

The new program hooked into the familiar packet filter via a set of special-purpose tables and redirection rules. The basic design is easy to grasp, and based on our recent exposure to PF rule sets, understanding the following *pf.conf* lines should be straightforward:

```
table <spamd> persist
table <spamd-white> persist
rdr pass on $ext_if inet proto tcp from <spamd> to \
        { $ext_if, $localnet } port smtp -> 127.0.0.1 port 8025
rdr pass on $ext_if inet proto tcp from !<spamd-white> to \
        { $ext_if, $localnet } port smtp -> 127.0.0.1 port 8025
```

We have two tables with distinctive names. For now we'll just note the names and move on. The crucial part is that SMTP traffic from the addresses in the first table plus the ones that *are not* in the second table are redirected to a daemon listening at port 8025.

Remember, You Are Not Alone: Blacklisting

The main point underlying the original spamd design is the fact that spammers send a large number of messages, and the probability that you are the first person receiving a particular message is incredibly small. In addition, spam is mainly sent via a few spammer-friendly networks and a large number of hijacked machines. Both the individual messages and the machines will be reported to blacklists fairly quickly, and this is the data that eventually ends up in the first table in our example.

Classic spamd: Blacklists and the Sticky Tar Pit

In the classic mode, spamd employs a method called *tarpitting*. The daemon presents its banner to SMTP connections from addresses in the blacklist and then immediately switches to a mode where it answers SMTP traffic one byte at a time, intending to waste as much time as possible on the sending end while costing the receiver pretty much nothing.

The specific implementation with 1-byte SMTP replies is often referred to as *stuttering*. Blacklist-based tarpitting with stuttering was the default mode for spamd up to and including OpenBSD 4.0.

Setting up spamd to run in traditional, blacklisting-only mode is fairly straightforward. Start by putting the redirections and table definitions just mentioned in your *pf.conf* file, and then turn your attention to the *spamd.conf* file.

NOTE *Note that on FreeBSD, spamd is a port,* mail/spamd/. *If you are running PF on FreeBSD 5.x or newer, you need to install the port, follow the directions given by the port's messages, and then return here.*

A Basic spamd.conf File

As distributed, the file itself offers quite a bit of explanation, and the man page offers additional information, but we will recap the essentials here.

NOTE *On OpenBSD 4.0 and earlier (and by extension, ports that are based on versions prior to OpenBSD 4.1),* spamd.conf *was in* /etc. *Starting with OpenBSD 4.1, the file is to be found in the* /etc/mail *directory instead.*

Near the beginning of the file, you will notice a line without a # comment sign that says all:\. This line specifies the lists you actually use, such as

```
all:\
:uatraps:whitelist:
```

Here you add all blacklists you want to use, separated by colons (:). If you want to use whitelists to subtract addresses from your blacklist, add the name of the whitelist immediately after the name of each blacklist, for example, :blacklist:whitelist:.

Next up is a blacklist definition:

```
uatraps:\
        :black:\
        :msg="SPAM. Your address %A has sent spam within the last 24 hours":\
        :method=http:\
        :file=www.openbsd.org/spamd/traplist.gz
```

Following the name, the first data field specifies the list type, in this case black. The msg field contains the message displayed to blacklisted senders during the SMTP dialog. The method field specifies how the spamd-setup program fetches the list data, in this case http. Other possibilities include fetching via ftp, from a file in a mounted filesystem, or via exec of an external program. Finally, the file field specifies the name of the file spamd expects to receive.

The definition of a whitelist, as shown below, follows much the same pattern but omits the message parameter, since a message is not needed:

```
whitelist:\
        :white:\
        :method=file:\
        :file=/var/mail/whitelist.txt
```

WARNING *Choose your data sources with care. The suggested blacklists in the default* spamd.conf *as distributed could potentially exclude quite large blocks of the Internet, including several address ranges that claim to cover entire countries. It goes pretty much without saying that if your site expects to exchange legitimate email with any of the countries in question, those lists may not be optimal for your setup. Other popular lists have been known to list entire /16 ranges as spam sources, and it is well worth the effort to find out the details of the list's maintenance policy before putting a blacklist into production. You are the judge of which data sources to use, and using lists other than the default ones is possible.*

Put the lines for spamd and the startup parameters you want in your */etc/rc.conf* or */etc/rc.conf.local.* For example, this line

```
spamd_flags="-v" # for normal use: "" and see spamd-setup(8)
```

enables spamd to run in blacklisting mode on OpenBSD 4.0 and earlier. The -v flag enables verbose logging, which is useful for keeping track of spamd's activity for debugging.

NOTE *If you want spamd to run in pure blacklist mode without greylisting (described in the next section) on OpenBSD 4.1 or newer, set the* spamd_black *variable to* YES *and then restart* spamd *to turn off greylisting and enable blacklisting-only mode.*

When you have finished editing the setup, start spamd with the options you want and complete the configuration using spamd-setup. Finally, create a cron job that calls spamd-setup to update the tables at reasonable intervals.

By default, spamd logs to your general system logs. If you want the spamd log messages to go to a separate log file to reduce the clutter in your system logs, you may want to add an entry similar to this to your *syslog.conf* file:

```
!!spamd
daemon.err;daemon.warn;daemon.info                        /var/log/spamd
```

When you're satisfied that spamd is running and does what it is supposed to do, you will probably want to add the spamd log file to your log rotations, too.

Once spamd-setup has been run and the tables are filled, you can view table contents using pfctl or other applications. If you want to change or delete entries, you are advised to use the spamdb utility instead of pfctl table commands. (We'll talk more about that later.)

Note that in the example *pf.conf* fragment at the beginning of "Giving Spammers a Hard Time with spamd" on page 72, the redirection (rdr) rules are also pass rules. If your rdr rules do not include a pass part, you need to set up pass rules to let traffic through to your redirection target. You also need to set up rules to let legitimate email through. If you are already running an email service on your network, you can probably go on using your old SMTP pass rules.

Pure blacklisting mode is here mostly for historical reasons. Given a set of reliable and well-maintained blacklists, it does a good job of keeping known spam-sending machines occupied. However, the real gains in spam prevention come with greylisting, which is a crucial part of how the modern spamd works.

Greylisting: My Admin Told Me Not to Talk to Strangers

Greylisting consists mainly of interpreting the current SMTP standards with a reasonable helping of pedantry and then adding a little white lie to make life easier.

Spammers tend to use other people's equipment to send their messages, and the software they install without the legal owner's permission needs to be relatively lightweight to be able to run undetected. There are also strong indications that spammers typically do not consider any individual message they send to be important. Taken together, this means that typical spam and malware sender software is probably not set up to interpret SMTP status codes correctly.

We can use this to our advantage, as Evan Harris first showed in a 2003 paper.[1] The main point is, when a compromised machine is used to send spam, the sender application tends to try delivery only once, without checking for any results or return codes. Real SMTP implementations interpret SMTP return codes and act on them, and real mail servers retry if the initial attempt fails with any kind of temporary error. The initial design and early test results seemed promising, and a number of greylisting implementations followed over the next few months after the paper appeared.

Even though Internet services are offered with no guarantees, usually described as *best-effort services*, a significant amount of design and development effort has been put into making essential services such as SMTP email transmission fault tolerant. In practical terms, this means that the best effort of a service such as SMTP is as close as you can get to having a perfect record for delivering messages. That's why we can rely on greylisting to eventually receive email from proper mail servers.

The current standard for Internet email transmission is defined in RFC 2821. In that document's section 4.5.4.1, "Sending Strategy," we find that

> In a typical system, the program that composes a message has some method for requesting immediate attention for a new piece of outgoing mail, while mail that cannot be transmitted immediately MUST be queued and periodically retried by the sender.

and

> The sender MUST delay retrying a particular destination after one attempt has failed. In general, the retry interval SHOULD be at least 30 minutes; however, more sophisticated and variable strategies will be beneficial when the SMTP client can determine the reason for non-delivery.

RFC 2821 then goes on to state that

> Retries continue until the message is transmitted or the sender gives up; the give-up time generally needs to be at least 4–5 days.

---

[1] The original Harris paper and a number of other useful articles and resources can be found at *http://www.greylisting.org*.

To summarize, delivering email is a collaborative, best-effort process, and the RFC clearly states that if the site you are trying to send email to reports it can't receive anything at the moment, it is your *duty* (a *must* requirement) to try again later, giving the receiving server a chance to recover from its problem.

The clever wrinkle to greylisting is that it's a convenient white lie. When we claim to have a temporary local problem, the temporary local problem is really the equivalent of *My admin told me not to talk to strangers*. Well-behaved senders with valid messages will come calling again later, but spammers have no interest in waiting around for the chance to retry, since it would increase their cost of delivering the messages.

This is the essence of why greylisting still works. And since it's really a matter of being slightly pedantic about following accepted standards,[2] false positives are very rare.

OpenBSD's spamd acquired its ability to greylist in OpenBSD 3.5, which was released in May 2004. Starting with OpenBSD 4.1, which was released May 1, 2007, spamd runs in greylisting mode by default.

The most amazing thing about greylisting, apart from its simplicity, is that it still works. Spammers and malware writers have been very slow to adapt. We will see a few examples later.

Setting Up spamd in Greylisting Mode

With the necessary rules in place in your *pf.conf*, configuring spamd for greylisting is fairly straightforward.

SPAMD ON FREEBSD NEEDS FDESCFS

Note that on FreeBSD, to use spamd in greylisting mode you need to have a file descriptor filesystem (see man 5 fdescfs) mounted at */dev/fd/*. You can do this by adding the following line to your */etc/fstab*:

```
fdescfs /dev/fd fdescfs rw 0 0
```

The fdescfs code is available as a loadable kernel module in the default configuration, but if you are using a custom kernel, you may need to check that the module is available or that the code is compiled in.

Begin by placing the lines for spamd and the startup parameters you want in your */etc/rc.conf* or */etc/rc.conf.local*, for example:

```
spamd_flags="-v -G 2:4:864" # for normal use: "" and see spamd-setup(8)
spamd_grey=YES              # use spamd greylisting if YES
```

---

[2] The relevant RFCs are mainly RFC 1123 and RFC 2821. If you choose to join us greylisting pedants, you will need to read these, if only for proper RFC-style background information. Remember, temporary rejection is in fact an SMTP fault-tolerance feature.

Once again, on OpenBSD 4.1 and later, the `spamd_grey` variable is superfluous, since greylisting is the default mode.[3]

Note that you can fine-tune several of the greylisting-related parameters via spamd command-line parameters trailing the `-G` option. This colon-separated list consists of the values `passtime`, `greyexp`, and `whiteexp`. Here `passtime` denotes the minimum number of minutes spamd considers a reasonable time before retry. The default is 25 minutes, but in this configuration this has been reduced to 2 minutes. Both `greyexp` and `whiteexp` are measured in hours, where `greyexp` is the number of hours an entry stays in the greylisted state before it is removed from the database, and `whiteexp` is how long a whitelisted entry is kept around. The default values are 4 hours and 864 hours (just over one month), respectively.

Tracking Your Real Mail Connections: spamlogd

Behind the scenes, rarely mentioned, and barely documented is one of spamd's most important helper programs: the `spamlogd` whitelist updater. As the name suggests, `spamlogd` works quietly in the background, recording logged connections to and from your mail servers to keep your whitelist updated. The idea is to make sure valid email to and from hosts you communicate with regularly goes through with a minimum of fuss.

NOTE *Restart spamd to enable greylisting. If you followed the natural progression up to this point, it's most likely spamlogd has been started automatically already. However, if your initial spamd configuration did not include greylisting, spamlogd may not have been started, and you may experience strange symptoms such as the greylist and whitelist not getting updated properly. Under normal circumstances, you should not have to start spamlogd by hand. Restarting spamd after you have enabled greylisting ensures that spamlogd is loaded and available too.*

In order to perform its job properly, `spamlogd` needs you to log SMTP connections to and from your mail servers, such as in the sample rule set discussed earlier in this chapter:

```
emailserver = "192.0.2.225"
pass log proto tcp from any to $emailserver port $email synproxy state
pass log proto tcp from $emailserver to any port smtp synproxy state
```

On OpenBSD 4.1 and later (and equivalents), you can create several pflog interfaces and specify which interface a rule should log to. If you want to separate the data `spamlogd` needs to read from the rest of your PF logs, create a separate pflog1 interface using `ifconfig pflog1 create` or by making a *hostname.pflog1* file that contains only the line up. If you change the rules to

```
pass log (to pflog1) proto tcp from any to $emailserver port $email
pass log (to pflog1) proto tcp from $emailserver to any port smtp
```

---

[3] As we mentioned in "A Basic spamd.conf File" on page 73, you can use the `spamd_black` variable to turn greylisting off.

and add `-l pflog1` to `spamlogd`'s startup parameters, you have separated the spamd-related logging from the rest. See Chapter 8 for more about logging.

With these rules in place, `spamlogd` will add the IP addresses that receive email you send to the whitelist. This is not an ironclad guarantee that the reply will pass immediately, but in most configurations it helps speed things up significantly.

Manual Intervention with spamdb

There will be times when you need to view or change the contents of your blacklists, whitelist, or greylist. These records are located in the */var/db/ spamdb* database, and an administrator's main interface to managing those lists is `spamdb`.

Early versions of `spamdb` simply offered options to add whitelist entries to the database or update existing ones (`spamdb -a nn.mm.nn.mm`) and to delete whitelist entries (`spamdb -d nn.mm.nn.mm`) to compensate for either short-comings in the blacklists used or the effects of the greylisting algorithms.

In recent times, `spamdb` has been developed to offer some interesting features to support greytrapping. We will come back to greytrapping and other recent advances in a short while, but first we'll take a look at some field notes on how `spamd` performs.

Some Highlights of Day-to-Day spamd Use

What is `spamd` like in practical use? Users and administrators at sites that implement greylisting tend to agree that they get rid of most of their spam that way. We will start by seeing what it looks like according to log files and then come back with some data.

If you start `spamd` with the `-v` command-line option for verbose logging, the logs include a few more items of information in addition to the IP addresses. With verbose logging, a typical log excerpt looks like this:

```
Oct  2 19:53:21 delilah spamd[26905]: 65.210.185.131: connected (1/1), lists: spews1
Oct  2 19:55:04 delilah spamd[26905]: 83.23.213.115: connected (2/1)
Oct  2 19:55:05 delilah spamd[26905]: (GREY) 83.23.213.115: <gilbert@keyholes.net> ->
wkitp98zpu.fsf@datadok.no>
Oct  2 19:55:05 delilah spamd[26905]: 83.23.213.115: disconnected after 0 seconds.
Oct  2 19:55:05 delilah spamd[26905]: 83.23.213.115: connected (2/1)
Oct  2 19:55:06 delilah spamd[26905]: (GREY) 83.23.213.115: <gilbert@keyholes.net> ->
<wkitp98zpu.fsf@datadok.no>
Oct  2 19:55:06 delilah spamd[26905]: 83.23.213.115: disconnected after 1 seconds.
Oct  2 19:57:07 delilah spamd[26905]: (BLACK) 65.210.185.131: <bounce-3C7E40A4B3@branch15.summer-
bargainz.com> -> <adm@dataped.no>
Oct  2 19:58:50 delilah spamd[26905]: 65.210.185.131: From: Auto lnsurance Savings
<noreply@branch15.summer-bargainz.com>
Oct  2 19:58:50 delilah spamd[26905]: 65.210.185.131: Subject: Start SAVlNG MONEY on Auto
lnsurance
Oct  2 19:58:50 delilah spamd[26905]: 65.210.185.131: To: adm@dataped.no
Oct  2 20:00:05 delilah spamd[26905]: 65.210.185.131: disconnected after 404 seconds. lists:
spews1
```

```
Oct  2 20:03:48 delilah spamd[26905]: 222.240.6.118: connected (1/0)
Oct  2 20:03:48 delilah spamd[26905]: 222.240.6.118: disconnected after 0 seconds.
Oct  2 20:06:51 delilah spamd[26905]: 24.71.110.10: connected (1/1), lists: spews1
Oct  2 20:07:00 delilah spamd[26905]: 221.196.37.249: connected (2/1)
Oct  2 20:07:00 delilah spamd[26905]: 221.196.37.249: disconnected after 0 seconds.
Oct  2 20:07:12 delilah spamd[26905]: 24.71.110.10: disconnected after 21 seconds. lists: spews1
```

The first line is the beginning of a connection from a machine in the
spews1 blacklist. The next six lines show the complete records of two connection attempts from another machine, which each time connects as the second
active connection. This second machine is not yet in any blacklist, so it is
greylisted.[4] The (GREY) or (BLACK) before the addresses indicates greylisting
or blacklisting status. Then there is more activity from the blacklisted host,
and a little later we see that after 404 seconds (or 6 minutes, 44 seconds), the
blacklisted host gives up without completing the delivery. The remaining
lines show a few very short connections, including one more from a machine
that is already in a blacklist. This time, though, the machine disconnects too
quickly to see any (BLACK) flag at the beginning of the SMTP dialog, but we
see a reference to the list name (spews1) at the end.

Roughly 400 seconds is about par for naïve spam senders that end up
in blacklists to hang around, according to data from various sites. That also
corresponds roughly to the time it takes—at the rate of 1 byte per second—
to complete the MAIL TO: ... dialog until spamd rejects the message back to
the sender's queue. However, while peeking at the logs, you are likely to
find some that hang around significantly longer. In the data from our office
gateway, one log entry stood out for a long time:

```
Dec 11 23:57:24 delilah spamd[32048]: 69.6.40.26: connected (1/1), lists: spamhaus spews1
spews2
Dec 12 00:30:08 delilah spamd[32048]: 69.6.40.26: disconnected after 1964 seconds. lists:
spamhaus spews1 spews2
```

This particular machine was already on several blacklists when it made
13 attempts at delivery between December 9 and December 12, 2004. The
last attempt lasted 32 minutes, 44 seconds, without completing the delivery.
However, most connections are a lot shorter than this. The relatively intelligent spam senders drop the connection during the first few seconds, like
the ones in the first log fragment. Others give up after around 400 seconds,
while a very small number hang on for hours.[5]

These days, most sites have some sort of content filtering in place to
handle spam and email-borne malware. Sites that complement their setup
with a spamd on their gateway see the load on the content-filtering machines
drop significantly.

---

[4] Note the rather curious delivery address (*wkitp98zpu.fsf@datadok.no*) in the message that the
greylisted machine tries to deliver here. There is a useful trick that we'll look at in "Setting Up
Your Own Traplist" on page 81.

[5] The most extreme case we have recorded hung on for 42,673 seconds, which is almost
12 hours. See Appendix A for references to other publications and more data.

Harvesting the Noise: The Fundamentals of Greytrapping

By the time the development cycle for OpenBSD 3.8 started during the first half of 2005, spamd users and developers had accumulated significant amounts of data and experience on spammer behavior and reactions to countermeasures.

We already know that spam senders rarely use a fully compliant SMTP implementation to send their messages—that's why greylisting works. Also, as we noted earlier, not only do spammers send large numbers of messages, they rarely check that the addresses they feed to their hijacked machines are actually deliverable. Combine these facts, and you'll see that if a grey-listed machine tries to send a message to an invalid address in your domain, there is a significant probability that the message is spam or, for that matter, malware.

Enter Greytrapping

Consequently, spamd had to learn greytrapping. Greytrapping as implemented in spamd is quite simple and, to my mind, quite elegant. The main thing we need as a starting point is a spamd that runs in greylisting mode. The other crucial component is a list of addresses in domains our servers handle email for, but only addresses that we are quite sure will never receive any legitimate email. How many addresses are in your list is not important. There needs to be at least one, and the upper limit is mainly defined by how many addresses you feel inclined to add.

Next up, use spamdb to feed your list into spamd's greytrapping feature, and sit back to watch. At first contact, a sender trying to send email to an address on your greytrap list is simply greylisted, like any other we have not exchanged email with before.

If the same machine tries again later, either retrying to the same invalid address as earlier or trying to deliver to one of the other addresses on your greytrapping list, the greytrap is triggered. The offender is then put into a temporary blacklist, dubbed spamd-greytrap, for 24 hours. For the next 24 hours, any SMTP traffic from the greytrapped host will be stuttered at, with one-byte-at-a-time replies.

Twenty-four hours is short enough to not cause serious disruption of legitimate traffic, since real SMTP implementations will keep trying to deliver for a few days, at least.

Experience from large-scale implementations of the technique shows that it rarely, if ever, produces false positives. Machines that continue spamming after 24 hours will make it back to the tar pit soon enough.

One prime example of useful greytrapping is Bob Beck's *ghosts of usenet postings past*–based traplist, generated automatically by computers running spamd at the University of Alberta, which rarely contains less than 20,000 IP address entries. The number of hosts varies widely and has been as high as roughly 175,000. At the time this book was written (November 2007), the list typically contained around 110,000 entries. While still officially in testing, it was made publicly available on January 30, 2006. To my knowledge, the list has yet to produce any false positives and is available from *http://www.openbsd .org/spamd/traplist.gz* for your *spamd.conf*.[6]

Setting Up Your Own Traplist

To set up your own traplist, use `spamdb`'s -T option. In my case, the strange address I mentioned earlier was a natural candidate for inclusion:[7]

```
$ sudo spamdb -T -a wkitp98zpu.fsf@datadok.no
```

That address is completely bogus. I use the GNUS email and news client, and this looks very much like the kind of message-ID the program generates. That message-ID was probably lifted from a news spool or some unfortunate malware victim's mailbox. But sure enough, the spammers thought this was just as usable as it was almost two years earlier. As you'll see, the same delivery address is being recycled.

```
Nov  6 09:50:25 delilah spamd[23576]: 210.214.12.57: connected (1/0)
Nov  6 09:50:32 delilah spamd[23576]: 210.214.12.57: connected (2/0)
Nov  6 09:50:40 delilah spamd[23576]: (GREY) 210.214.12.57: <gilbert@keyholes.net> ->
<wkitp98zpu.fsf@datadok.no>
Nov  6 09:50:40 delilah spamd[23576]: 210.214.12.57: disconnected after 15 seconds.
Nov  6 09:50:42 delilah spamd[23576]: 210.214.12.57: connected (2/0)
Nov  6 09:50:45 delilah spamd[23576]: (GREY) 210.214.12.57: <bounce-3C7E40A4B3@branch15.summer-
bargainz.com> -> <adm@datadok.no>
Nov  6 09:50:45 delilah spamd[23576]: 210.214.12.57: disconnected after 13 seconds.
Nov  6 09:50:50 delilah spamd[23576]: 210.214.12.57: connected (2/0)
Nov  6 09:51:00 delilah spamd[23576]: (GREY) 210.214.12.57: <gilbert@keyholes.net> ->
<wkitp98zpu.fsf@datadok.no>
Nov  6 09:51:00 delilah spamd[23576]: 210.214.12.57: disconnected after 18 seconds.
Nov  6 09:51:02 delilah spamd[23576]: 210.214.12.57: connected (2/0)
Nov  6 09:51:02 delilah spamd[23576]: 210.214.12.57: disconnected after 12 seconds.
Nov  6 09:51:02 delilah spamd[23576]: 210.214.12.57: connected (2/0)
Nov  6 09:51:18 delilah spamd[23576]: (GREY) 210.214.12.57: <gilbert@keyholes.net> ->
<wkitp98zpu.fsf@datadok.no>
Nov  6 09:51:18 delilah spamd[23576]: 210.214.12.57: disconnected after 16 seconds.
Nov  6 09:51:18 delilah spamd[23576]: (GREY) 210.214.12.57: <bounce-3C7E40A4B3@branch15.summer-
bargainz.com> -> <adm@dataped.no>
Nov  6 09:51:18 delilah spamd[23576]: 210.214.12.57: disconnected after 16 seconds.
Nov  6 09:51:20 delilah spamd[23576]: 210.214.12.57: connected (1/1), lists: spamd-greytrap
Nov  6 09:51:23 delilah spamd[23576]: 210.214.12.57: connected (2/2), lists: spamd-greytrap
Nov  6 09:55:33 delilah spamd[23576]: (BLACK) 210.214.12.57: <gilbert@keyholes.net> ->
<wkitp98zpu.fsf@datadok.no>
Nov  6 09:55:34 delilah spamd[23576]: (BLACK) 210.214.12.57: <bounce-
3C7E40A4B3@branch15.summer-bargainz.com> -> <adm@dataped.no>
```

---

[6] This list is part of recent sample *spamd.conf* files as the `uatraps` blacklist. In addition to this list, Bob recommends using *heise.de*'s nixspam list, also in the sample *spamd.conf* file, which is generated from various sources with a four-day automatic expiry. Detailed information about that list is available from Heise's website at *http://www.heise.de/ix/nixspam/dnsbl_en*.

[7] The actual command I entered back then was $ sudo spamdb -T -a "<wkitp98zpu.fsf@datadok.no>". In OpenBSD 4.1 and later, `spamdb` does not require the angle brackets or quotes, but it will accept them if you put them in.

This log fragment shows how the spammer's machine is greylisted at first contact and then clumsily tries to deliver messages to the curious address I added to my traplist, only to end up in the spamd-greytrap blacklist after a few minutes. By now we all know what it will be doing for the next 20-odd hours.

On a side note, it looks like even though the spammer moved to a different machine to send from, both the From: and To: addresses stayed the same. The fact that it's still trying to send to an address that has never been deliverable is a strong indicator that this spammer outfit does not check its lists too frequently. By the time you read this, it might be worth checking to see if the sender domain is still registered. At the time of this writing, it does not receive email and is clearly marked as being for sale.

Deleting and Handling Trapped Entries

There are a few more spamdb options you should be aware of. The -T option combined with -d lets you delete traplist email address entries, while the -t (lowercase) option combined with -a or -d lets you add or delete trapped IP address entries from the database.

Exporting your list of currently trapped addresses can be as simple as putting together a one-liner with spamdb, grep, and a little imagination.

Keeping Several spamd Greylists in Sync

Starting with OpenBSD 4.1, spamd is able to keep the greylisting databases in sync across any number of cooperating greylisting gateways.

The implementation is via a set of spamd command-line options: the -Y option specifies a *sync target*, that is, the IP address(es) of other spamd-running gateways you want to inform of updates to your greylisting information. On the receiving end, the -y option specifies a *sync listener*, which is the address or interface where this spamd instance is prepared to receive greylisting updates from other hosts.

Our main spamd gateway, *mainoffice-gw.example.com*, might have the following options added to its startup command line to establish a sync target and sync listening, respectively:

```
-Y minorbranch-gw.example.com -y mainoffice-gw.example.com
```

Conversely, *minorbranch-gw.example.com* at the branch office would have the hostnames reversed, as shown below:

```
-Y mainoffice-gw.example.com -y minorbranch-gw.example.com
```

Note that spamd also supports shared-secret authentication between the synchronization partners. If you create the file */etc/mail/spamd.key* and distribute copies of that file to all synchronization partners, the contents of that file will be used to calculate the necessary checksums for authentication. The file itself can be any kind of data, such as random data harvested from */dev/arandom*, as suggested by spamd's man page.

Detecting Out-of-Order MX Use

Another nice feature that was introduced in OpenBSD 4.1 was spamd's ability to detect out-of-order MX use. Contacting a secondary email exchanger first instead of trying the main one is a fairly well-known spammer trick and one that runs contrary to the behavior we expect from ordinary email transfer agents.

In other words, if someone tries the email exchangers in the wrong order, it's pretty much certain that he or she is trying to deliver spam. For our *example.com* domain, where the main mail server has the IP address 192.0.2.225 and the backup has the address 192.0.2.224, adding -M 192.0.2.224 to spamd's startup options would mean that any host that tries to contact 192.0.2.224 via SMTP before contacting the main mail server at 192.0.2.225 would be added to the local spamd-greytrap list to sweat it out for the next 24 hours.

Handling Sites That Do Not Play Well with Greylisting

Unfortunately, there are situations in which you will need to compensate for the peculiarities of other sites' email setups. We have already learned that the main reason greylisting works is that any standards-compliant email setup is required to retry delivery after some *reasonable* amount of time. However, as Murphy will be all too happy to tell you, life is not always that simple.

For one thing, the first email message sent from any site that has not contacted you for as long as the greylister keeps its data around will be delayed for some random amount of time, which depends mainly on the sender's retry interval.

Under some circumstances, even a minimal delay is undesirable. If, for example, you have some infrequent customers who always demand immediate and urgent attention to their business when they do contact you, an initial delivery delay of what could be up to several hours may not be optimal.

In addition, you are bound to encounter misconfigured mail servers that either do not retry at all or retry too quickly, perhaps stopping delivery retries after a few attempts or even just one.

Finally, there are some sites that are large enough to have several outgoing SMTP servers and do not play well with greylisting, since they are not guaranteed to retry delivery of any given message from the same IP address as the last delivery attempt for that message. Even though those sites can sincerely claim to comply with the retry requirements, since the RFCs do not state that the new delivery attempts *have to* come from the same IP address, it's fairly obvious that this is one of the few remaining downsides of greylisting.

If you need to compensate for such things in your setup, it is fairly easy to do. One useful approach is to define a table for a local whitelist to be fed from a file in case of reboots, as follows:

```
table <localwhite> file "/etc/mail/whitelist.txt"
```

To make sure SMTP traffic from the addresses in that table is not fed to spamd, add a `no rdr` rule at the top of your redirection block, as shown here:

```
no rdr proto tcp from <localwhite> to $mailservers port smtp
```

Once you have these changes added to your rule set, enter the addresses you need to protect from redirection into the *whitelist.txt* file and then reload your rule set using `pfctl -f /etc/pf.conf`. You can then use all the expected table tricks on the `<localwhite>` table, including replacing its content after editing the *whitelist.txt* file.

It is worth noting that at least some of the sites with many outgoing SMTP servers also publish information about which hosts are allowed to send email for their domain via SPF records,[8] which are part of the DNS information for the domain.

To retrieve the SPF records for our *example.com* domain, you could use the host command's `-ttxt` option, like this:

```
$ host -ttxt example.com
```

The command would produce an answer roughly like this:

```
example.com descriptive text "v=spf1 ip4:192.0.2.129/25 -all"
```

where the text in quotes is the *example.com* domain's SPF record. If you want email from *example.com* to arrive quickly, and you trust the people there not to send or relay spam, pick the address range from the SPF record, put it in your *whitelist.txt* file, and reload the `<localwhite>` table contents from the updated file.

Conclusions from Our spamd Experience

Summing up, selectively used blacklists combined with spamd are powerful, precise, and efficient spam-fighting tools. The load on the spamd machine is minimal. On the other hand, spamd will never perform better than its weakest data source, which means you will need to monitor your logs and use white-listing when necessary.

It is also perfectly feasible to run spamd in a pure greylisting mode, with no blacklists. In fact, some users report that a purely greylisting spamd config-uration is not significantly less effective than a blacklisting configuration as a spam-fighting tool and in some cases, it is significantly more effective than content filtering.

---

[8] SPF records are stored in DNS zones as special-purpose TXT records; see *http://www.openspf.org* for details. Note that here we use SPF only as a possible source of information. A full discussion of the pros and cons of the SPF architecture and its intended purpose is outside the scope of this book.

One such report is Steve Williams's October 20, 2006 message to the *OpenBSD-misc* mailing list,[9] where he reports that a pure greylisting configuration immediately rid the company he worked for of approximately 95 percent of its spam load.

From my own experience, I recommend using Bob Beck's traplist, generated by large-scale greytrapping, as the only imported blacklist. What makes this list stand out is that Bob set up the system to remove addresses automatically after 24 hours. This means that you get an extremely low number of false positives.

Once you're happy with your setup, you could try introducing local greytrapping. This is likely to catch a few more undesirables, and of course it's good, clean fun.

Some limited experiments, which were carried out while I was writing this chapter,[10] even suggest that harvesting the invalid addresses spammers use from your mail server logs, spamd logs, or directly from your greylist to put in your traplist is extremely efficient. Publishing the list on a moderately visible web page appears to ensure that the addresses you put there will be recorded over and over again by address-harvesting robots and will provide you with even better greytrapping material, since they are then more likely to be kept on the spammers' list of *known-good* addresses.

---

[9] Accessible (among other places) at *http://marc.info/?l=openbsd-misc&m=116136841831550&w=2.*

[10] Chronicled at *http://bsdly.blogspot.com,* entries starting with *http://bsdly.blogspot.com/2007/07/hey-spammer-heres-list-for-you.html.*

7

QUEUES, SHAPING, AND REDUNDANCY

This chapter deals with two main topics, which taken either separately or together have the potential to radically transform your networking experience. The common theme in this chapter is managing resource availability. In the first part of the chapter we look at how to use the ALTQ traffic-shaping subsystem to allocate bandwidth resources efficiently and according to a specified policy. The second part of the chapter explores how to make sure your resources stay available by using the redundancy features offered by the CARP and pfsync protocols.

Directing Traffic with ALTQ

ALTQ, short for *ALTernate Queuing*, is a very flexible mechanism for network traffic shaping, which had a life of its own before getting integrated into PF on OpenBSD.[1] On OpenBSD, ALTQ was integrated into the PF code for the

---

[1] The original research on ALTQ was presented in a paper for the USENIX 1999 conference. You can read Kenjiro Cho's paper "Managing Traffic with ALTQ" online at *http://www.usenix .org/publications/library/proceedings/usenix99/cho.html*.

OpenBSD 3.3 release, with the configuration done in *pf.conf* mainly because it makes sense to integrate traffic shaping and filtering. PF ports to other BSDs followed suit, with at least some optional ALTQ integration. The integration process is not yet complete in all systems, and we will look into some of the differences where they are relevant.

Basic ALTQ Concepts

Managing your bandwidth has a lot in common with balancing your checkbook or handling other resources that are either scarce or available in finite quantities. The resource is available in a constant supply with hard upper limits, and you need to allocate the resource with maximum *efficiency*, according to the *priorities* set out in your *policy* or *specification*.

The core of ALTQ bandwidth management is the queue concept. *Queues* are a form of buffer for network packets. They are where the packets are held until they are either dropped or sent on their way according to the criteria that apply to the queue; the packets are subject to the queue's available bandwidth. Queues are attached to specific interfaces, and bandwidth is managed on a per-interface basis, with available bandwidth on a given interface subdivided into the queues you define.

Queues are defined with either a specific amount of bandwidth or a specific portion of available bandwidth, and sometimes they have hierarchical priority. *Priority* in this context is an indicator of preference, or which queue should be serviced with the lowest delay. As we will see later, some queue types can even be configured with a combination of bandwidth allocation and priority. For even further refinement, some queue types let you allocate portions of each queue's bandwidth share to *subqueues*, or queues within queues, which share the parent queue's resources. Once queue definitions are in place, you integrate traffic shaping into your rule set by rewriting your pass rules to assign traffic to a specific queue. We'll cover this in more detail in the following pages.

NOTE *In ALTQ setups, any traffic that you do not explicitly assign to a specific queue gets lumped in with everything else in the default queue.*

Queue Schedulers, aka Queue Disciplines

In the default networking setup, with no ALTQ-style queuing, the TCP/IP stack and its filtering subsystem process the packets in order as they arrive on an interface. This is what we generally refer to as the *First In, First Out,* or *FIFO,* discipline.

ALTQ queues can be set up to behave quite differently, sometimes with startling effect. Each of the three queue scheduler algorithms, or *disciplines,* offers its own unique set of options:

priq

   Priority-based queues are defined purely in terms of priority within the total bandwidth. For priq queues, the allowed priority range is 0 through 15, where a higher value earns preferential treatment. Packets that match the criteria for higher-priority queues are serviced before the ones matching lower-priority queues.

cbq

Class-based queues are defined as constant-size bandwidth allocations, as a percentage of the total available or in units of kilobits, megabits, or gigabits per second. A cbq queue can be subdivided into queues, which are assigned priorities in the range of 0 to 7, and again, a higher priority means preferential treatment. Packets are kept in the queue until the bandwidth is available. For queues that are subdivided into queues with priority as well as bandwidth allocations, packets that match the criteria for a higher-priority queue are serviced sooner.

hfsc

This discipline uses the *Hierarchical Fair Service Curve (HFSC)* algorithm to ensure a "fair" allocation of bandwidth among the queues in a hierarchy. Both the algorithm and the corresponding setup are fairly complicated, with a number of tunable parameters. For that reason, most ALTQ practitioners stick with the simpler queue types, but the ones who claim to understand HFSC pretty much swear by it.

The general syntax for ALTQ queues in PF looks like this:

```
altq on interface type [options ... ] main_queue { sub_q1, sub_q2 ..}
  queue sub_q1 [ options ... ]
  queue sub_q2 [ options ... ] { subA, subB, ... }
[...]
pass [ ... ] queue sub_q1
pass [ ... ] queue sub_q2
```

Note that cbq and hfsc queues can have several levels of subqueues, while priq queues are essentially flat, with only one queue level. We will address syntax specifics for each type in later sections of the chapter.

Setting Up ALTQ

Enabling ALTQ so you can use the queuing logic in your rule sets may require some extra steps, depending on which operating system is your platform of choice.

ALTQ on OpenBSD

On OpenBSD, all supported queue disciplines are compiled into the *GENERIC* and *GENERIC.MP* kernels, so the only configuration you need to do involves editing your *pf.conf*.

ALTQ on FreeBSD

On FreeBSD, you need to check that your kernel has ALTQ and the ALTQ queue discipline options compiled in. The default FreeBSD *GENERIC* kernel does not have the ALTQ options enabled. The relevant options are listed here:

```
options     ALTQ
options     ALTQ_CBQ        # Class-Based Queuing (CBQ)
options     ALTQ_RED        # Random Early Detection (RED)
options     ALTQ_RIO        # RED In/Out
options     ALTQ_HFSC       # Hierarchical Packet Scheduler (HFSC)
options     ALTQ_PRIQ       # Priority Queuing (PRIQ)
options     ALTQ_NOPCC      # Required for SMP build
```

The ALTQ option is needed to enable ALTQ in the kernel, and on SMP systems, you will *also* need the ALTQ_NOPCC option. Depending on which types of queues you will be using, you need to enable at least of one of ALTQ_CBQ, ALTQ_PRIQ, or ALTQ_HFSC. Finally, you can enable the congestion-avoidance techniques *Random Early Detection (RED)* and *RED In/Out*, the ALTQ_RED and ALTQ_RIO options, respectively. See the *FreeBSD Handbook* for information on how to compile and install a custom kernel with these options.

ALTQ on NetBSD

As I am writing this chapter, ALTQ is in the process of being integrated in the NetBSD 4.0 PF implementation. Much like the case with FreeBSD, NetBSD's default *GENERIC* kernel configuration does not include the ALTQ-related options. However, the *GENERIC* configuration file comes with all relevant options commented out for easy inclusion. The main kernel options are as follows:

```
options     ALTQ        # Manipulate network interfaces' output queues
options     ALTQ_CBQ    # Class-Based Queuing
options     ALTQ_HFSC   # Hierarchical Fair Service Curve
options     ALTQ_PRIQ   # Priority Queuing
options     ALTQ_RED    # Random Early Detection
```

The ALTQ option is needed to enable ALTQ in the kernel. Depending on which types of queues you will be using, you need to enable at least of one of ALTQ_CBQ, ALTQ_PRIQ, or ALTQ_HFSC.

For pre-4.0 NetBSD versions, Peter Postma maintains a patch to enable PF/ALTQ functions. Up-to-date information on this, including how to get the ALTQ patch via pkgsrc, is available from his PF on NetBSD pages (*http:// nedbsd.nl/~ppostma/pf*) and the NetBSD PF documentation (*http://www.netbsd .org/Documentation/network/pf.html*).

Either way, by now you should have all the information you need to get an ALTQ-enabled system up and running.

With these preliminaries out of the way, you should be ready to look at some example network configurations with ALTQ.

Understanding Priority-Based Queues (priq)

The basic concept for priority-based queues (priq) is fairly straightforward and perhaps the easiest one to understand. Within the total bandwidth allocated to the main queue, all that matters is traffic priority. You assign queues a priority value in the range 0 through 15, where a higher value means that the queue's requests for traffic are serviced sooner.

For a real-world example, we can look to Daniel Hartmeier. He discovered a simple yet effective way to improve the throughput for his home network by using ALTQ. Like many people, Daniel's home network was on an asymmetric connection, with total usable bandwidth low enough that he felt a strong desire to get better bandwidth utilization.

In addition, when the line was running at or near capacity, some oddities started appearing. One symptom in particular seemed to indicate that there was room for improvement: Incoming traffic (downloads, incoming email, and such) slowed down disproportionately whenever outgoing traffic started, more than could be explained by measuring the raw amount of data transferred. It all came back to a basic feature of TCP.

When a TCP packet is sent, the sender expects acknowledgment (in the form of an ACK packet) from the receiving end and will wait for a specified time for it to arrive. If the ACK does not arrive within the specified time, the sender assumes that the packet has not been received and resends the packet it originally sent.

The problem is that, in a default setup, packets are serviced sequentially by the interface as they arrive. This inevitably means that the ACK packets, with essentially no data payload, wait in line while the larger data packets are transferred.

A testable hypothesis formed: If the tiny, practically dataless ACK packets were able to slip in between the larger data packets, this would lead to a more efficient use of available bandwidth. The simplest practical way to implement and test the theory was to set up two queues with different priorities and integrate them into the rule set.

These lines show the relevant parts of the rule set:

```
ext_if="kue0"

altq on $ext_if priq bandwidth 100Kb queue { q_pri, q_def }
    queue q_pri priority 7
    queue q_def priority 1 priq(default)

pass out on $ext_if proto tcp from $ext_if to any flags S/SA \
        keep state queue (q_def, q_pri)

pass in  on $ext_if proto tcp from any to $ext_if flags S/SA \
        keep state queue (q_def, q_pri)
```

Here we see that the priority-based queue is set up on the external interface, with two subordinate queues. The first subqueue, q_pri, has a high priority value of 7, while the other, q_def, has a significantly lower priority value of 1.

This seemingly simple rule set works by exploiting how ALTQ treats queues with different priorities. Once a connection is assigned to the main queue, ALTQ inspects each packet's type of service (ToS) field. ACK packets have the ToS Delay bit set to low, which indicates that the sender wanted the speediest delivery possible. When ALTQ sees a low-delay packet and queues of differing priorities are available, it will assign the packet to the higher-priority queue.

This means that the ACK packets skip ahead of the lower-priority queue and are delivered more quickly, which in turn means that data packets are serviced more quickly too. The net result is that a configuration like this provides better performance than a pure FIFO configuration with the same hardware and available bandwidth.[2]

---

[2] Daniel's article about this version of his setup at *http://www.benzedrine.cx/ackpri.html* contains a more detailed analysis.

Class-Based Bandwidth Allocation for Small Networks (cbq)

Maximizing network performance generally feels nice. However, you may find that your network has other needs. For example, it might be important that some traffic such as email and other vital services has a baseline amount of bandwidth available at all times, while other services (peer-to-peer file sharing comes to mind) should not be allowed to consume more than a certain amount. For addressing these kinds of requirements or concerns, the class-based queue (cbq) discipline offers a slightly larger set of options.

To illustrate how to use cbq, we'll move on to another example, which builds on the rule sets from previous chapters. We want to let the users on a small local network connect to a predefined set of services outside their own network and also allow access from the outside to a webserver somewhere on the local network.

Here all queues are set up on the external, Internet-facing interface. This approach makes sense mainly because bandwidth is more likely to be limited on the external link than on the local network. In principle, however, allocating queues and running traffic shaping can be done on any network interface. Here, the setup includes a cbq queue for a total bandwidth of 2 megabits with six subqueues.

```
altq on $ext_if cbq bandwidth 2Mb queue { main, ftp, udp, web, ssh, icmp }
    queue main bandwidth 18% cbq(default borrow red)
    queue ftp bandwidth 10% cbq(borrow red)
    queue udp bandwidth 30% cbq(borrow red)
    queue web bandwidth 20% cbq(borrow red)
    queue ssh bandwidth 20% cbq(borrow red) { ssh_interactive, ssh_bulk }
        queue ssh_interactive priority 7 bandwidth 20%
        queue ssh_bulk priority 0 bandwidth 80%
    queue icmp bandwidth 2% cbq
```

We see the subqueue main with 18 percent of the bandwidth designated as the default queue. This means any traffic that matches a pass rule but is not explicitly assigned to some other queue ends up here. The borrow and red keywords mean that the queue may "borrow" bandwidth from its parent queue, while the system attempts to avoid congestion by applying the RED algorithm.

The other queues follow more or less the same pattern, up to the subqueue ssh, which itself has two subqueues with separate priorities. Here we see a variation on the ACK priority example: Bulk SSH transfers, typically SCP file transfers, are transmitted with a ToS indicating throughput, while interactive SSH traffic has the ToS flag set to low delay and skips ahead of the bulk transfers. The interactive traffic is likely to be less bandwidth consuming and gets a smaller share of the bandwidth, but it gets preferential treatment because of the higher-priority value assigned to it.

This scheme also helps the speed of SCP file transfers, since the ACK packets for the SCP transfers will be assigned to the higher-priority subqueue.

Finally, we have the icmp queue, which is reserved for the remaining two percent of the bandwidth, from the top level. This guarantees a minimum amount of bandwidth for ICMP traffic that we want to pass but that does not match the criteria for being assigned to the other queues.

To make it all happen we use pass rules that show which traffic is assigned to the queues and their criteria:

```
set skip on { lo0, $int_if }
pass log quick on $ext_if proto tcp from any to any port ssh flags S/SA \
    keep state queue (ssh_bulk, ssh_interactive)
pass in quick on $ext_if proto tcp from any to any port ftp flags S/SA \
    keep state queue ftp
pass in quick on $ext_if proto tcp from any to any port www flags S/SA \
    keep state queue http
pass out on $ext_if proto udp all keep state queue udp
pass out on $ext_if proto icmp all keep state queue icmp
pass out on $ext_if proto tcp from $localnet to any port $client_out
```

The rules for ssh, ftp, www, udp, and icmp all assign traffic to their respective queues, while the last catch-all rule passes all other traffic from the local net, lumping it into the default main queue.

Queuing for Servers in a DMZ

Back in "A Degree of Physical Separation: Introducing the DMZ" on page 49, we set up a network with a single gateway but with all externally visible services configured on a separate DMZ network. That way, all traffic to the servers from both the Internet and the internal network has to pass through the gateway.

The network schematic is like Figure 7-1, which is identical to Figure 5-2.

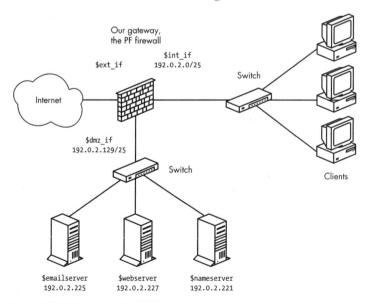

Figure 7-1: Network with DMZ

With the rule set from Chapter 5 as the starting point, we will be adding some queuing in order to optimize our network resources. The physical and logical layout of the network will not change.

The most likely bottleneck for this network is the bandwidth for the connection between the gateway's external interface and the Internet at large. The bandwidth elsewhere in our setup is not infinite, of course, but the available bandwidth on any interface in the local network is likely to be less of a limiting factor than the bandwidth actually available for communication with the outside world. For services to be available with the best possible performance, we need to set up the queues so the bandwidth available at the site is made available to the traffic we want to allow.

In this context it is important to understand the difference between interface bandwidth and the actual bandwidth available to the family of connections we want to let through. In our example, it is likely that the interface bandwidth on the DMZ interface is either 100Mb or 1Gb, while the actual available bandwidth for connections from outside the local network is considerably smaller. This consideration shows up in our queue definitions, where you clearly see that the actual bandwidth available for external traffic is the main limitation in the queue setup.

```
total_ext = 2Mb
total_dmz = 100Mb
altq on $ext_if cbq bandwidth $total_ext queue { ext_main, ext_web, ext_udp, ext_mail, ext_ssh }
queue ext_main bandwidth 25% cbq(default borrow red) { ext_hi, ext_lo }
     queue ext_hi priority 7 bandwidth 20%
     queue ext_lo priority 0 bandwidth 80%
queue ext_web bandwidth 25% cbq(borrow red)
queue ext_udp bandwidth 20% cbq(borrow red)
queue ext_mail bandwidth 30% cbq(borrow red)
altq on $dmz_if cbq bandwidth $total_dmz queue { ext_dmz, dmz_main, dmz_web, dmz_udp, dmz_mail }
queue ext_dmz bandwidth $total_ext cbq(borrow red) queue { ext_dmz_web, ext_dmz_udp, ext_dmz_mail }
     queue ext_dmz_web bandwidth 40% priority 5
     queue ext_dmz_udp bandwidth 10% priority 7
     queue ext_dmz_mail bandwidth 50% priority 3
queue dmz_main bandwidth 25Mb cbq(default borrow red) queue { dmz_main_hi, dmz_main_lo }
     queue dmz_main_hi priority 7 bandwidth 20%
     queue dmz_main_lo priority 0 bandwidth 80%
queue dmz_web bandwidth 25Mb cbq(borrow red)
queue dmz_udp bandwidth 20Mb cbq(borrow red)
queue dmz_mail bandwidth 20Mb cbq(borrow red)
```

Notice that the total_ext bandwidth limitation determines the allocation for all queues where the bandwidth for external connections is available. To make use of the new queuing infrastructure, we need to make some changes to the filtering rules, too. It is worth keeping in mind that any traffic you do not explicitly assign to a specific queue is assigned to the default queue for the interface. Thus, it is important to tune your filtering rules as well as your queue definitions to the actual traffic in your network.

The main part of the filtering rules could end up looking like this after adding the queues:

```
pass in on $ext_if proto { tcp, udp } from any to $nameservers port domain queue ext_udp
pass in on $int_if proto { tcp, udp } from $localnet to $nameservers port domain
pass out on $dmz_if proto { tcp, udp } from any to $nameservers port domain queue ext_dmz_udp
pass out on $dmz_if proto { tcp, udp } from $localnet to $nameservers port domain queue dmz_udp
pass in on $ext_if proto tcp from any to $webserver port $webports queue ext_web
pass in on $int_if proto tcp from $localnet to $webserver port $webports
pass out on $dmz_if proto tcp from any to $webserver port $webports queue ext_dmz_web
pass out on $dmz_if proto tcp from $localnet to $webserver port $webports queue dmz_web
pass in log on $ext_if proto tcp from any to $mailserver port smtp
pass in log on $ext_if proto tcp from $localnet to $mailserver port smtp
pass in log on $int_if proto tcp from $localnet to $mailserver port $email
pass out log on $dmz_if proto tcp from any to $mailserver port smtp queue ext_mail
pass in on $dmz_if from $mailserver to any port smtp queue dmz_mail
pass out log on $ext_if proto tcp from $mailserver to any port smtp queue ext_dmz_mail
```

You will notice that only traffic that will pass either the DMZ interface or the external interface is assigned to queues. In this configuration, with no externally accessible services on the internal network, queuing on the internal interface would not make much sense, since it is likely the part of our network with the least restrictions on available bandwidth.

Using ALTQ to Handle Unwanted Traffic

So far we have focused on queuing as a method to make sure specific kinds of traffic are let through as efficiently as possible, given the conditions that exist in and around your network. To wrap up our introduction to queuing, we'll take a look at some small examples that present a slightly different approach to identifying and handling unwanted traffic. These examples may help you reduce the noise level in your network a little by teaching you some queuing-related tricks you can use to keep miscreants in line.

Overloading to a Tiny Queue

Think back to "Turning Away the Brutes" on page 68, where we used a combination of state-tracking options and overload rules to fill up a table of addresses for special treatment. The special treatment we demonstrated in the previous chapter was to cut all connections, but it is equally possible to assign overload traffic to a specific queue instead.

Consider this rule from "Class-Based Bandwidth Allocation for Small Networks (cbq)" on page 93:

```
pass log quick on $ext_if proto tcp from any to any port ssh flags S/SA \
    keep state queue (ssh_bulk, ssh_interactive)
```

If we add state-tracking options, like this

```
pass log quick on $ext_if proto tcp from any to any port ssh flags S/SA \
    keep state (max-src-conn 15, max-src-conn-rate 5/3, \
    overload <bruteforce> flush global) queue (ssh_bulk, ssh_interactive)
```

and make one of the queues slightly smaller to make room for our overloaders, for example by making the web queue smaller and adding

```
queue smallpipe bandwidth 1% cbq
```

we can then assign traffic from miscreants to the small-bandwidth queue with the following rule:

```
pass inet proto tcp from <bruteforce> to any port $tcp_services queue smallpipe
```

It might also be useful to supplement rules like these with table entry expiry, as described in "Tidying Your Tables with pfctl" on page 70.

Queue Assignments Based on OS Fingerprints

PF has a fairly reliable operating system fingerprinting mechanism, which detects the operating system at the other end of a network connection based on characteristics of the initial SYN packets at connection setup. Our final ALTQ example expands on the previous simple rule set based on the common knowledge that machines that send spam are likely to run a particular operating system. If, for example, running spamd is not an option in your environment, a rule like this

```
pass quick proto tcp from any os "Windows" to $ext_if port smtp queue smallpipe
```

may be a simple substitute if you are quite sure nobody will ever be sending you legitimate email from systems running that particular operating system. Here, email traffic originating from hosts that run a particular operating system gets no more than 1 percent of your bandwidth, with no borrowing.

Redundancy and Failover: CARP and pfsync

High availability and uninterrupted service have been both marketing buzz-words and coveted goals for IT professionals and network administrators as long as most of us can remember. To meet this perceived need and solve a few related problems, CARP and pfsync were added as two highly anticipated features in OpenBSD 3.5.

Common Address Redundancy Protocol (CARP) was developed as a non–patent-encumbered alternative to *VRRP (Virtual Router Redundancy Protocol,* RFC 2281, RFC 3768), which was quite far along the track to becoming an IETF-sanctioned standard, even though possible patent issues have not been resolved.[3]

One of the main purposes of CARP is to ensure that the network will keep functioning as usual even when a firewall or other service goes down because of errors or planned maintenance activities such as upgrades. Complementing CARP, the pfsync protocol is designed to handle synchronization of PF states between redundant packet-filtering nodes or gateways. Both protocols are intended to ensure redundancy for essential network features with automatic failover.

CARP is based on setting up a group of machines as one *master* and one or more redundant *backups*, all of which are equipped to handle a common IP address. If the master goes down, one of the backups will inherit the IP address. The handover from one CARP host to another may be authenticated, essentially by setting a shared secret, in practice much like a password.

In the case of PF firewalls, pfsync can be set up to handle the synchronization, and if this is done properly, active connections will be handed over without noticeable interruption. In essence, pfsync is a type of virtual network interface specially designed to synchronize state information between PF firewalls. Its interfaces are assigned to physical interfaces with ifconfig. On networks where uptime requirements are strict enough to dictate automatic failover, the number of simultaneous network connections and accompanying state table changes is likely to be large enough that it will make sense to assign the pfsync network its own physical network. In addition, since pfsync does not perform any authentication on its synchronization partners, you can guarantee correct synchronization only if you are using dedicated interfaces for your pfsync traffic.

The Project Specification: A Redundant Pair of Gateways

Before we lose ourselves entirely in the vast array of options, now is a good time to set out the specification for the task at hand. In order to illustrate a useful failover setup with CARP and pfsync, let's imagine a network that at the moment has one gateway to the world.

The exact details of the PF rule set are not important at this point; more important is the goal of the exercise.

Our expectations are that after the reconfiguration is complete, the network should do the following things:

- Keep functioning much the same way as it did earlier
- Have better availability with no noticeable downtime
- Experience graceful failover with no interruption of active connections

---

[3] The patents involved are held by Cisco, IBM, and Nokia; see the RFCs for details.

We'll start with the relatively simple network from Chapter 3, which looks something like Figure 7-2.

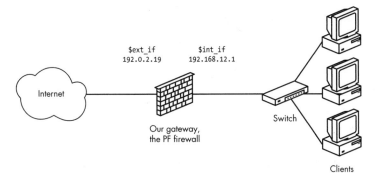

Figure 7-2: Network with a single gateway

We replace the single gateway with a redundant pair that shares a private network for state information updates over pfsync. The result is something like Figure 7-3.

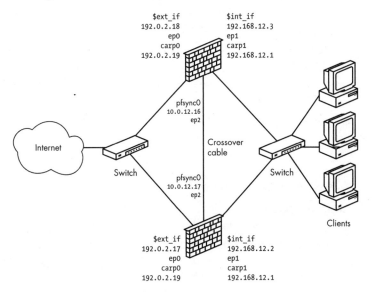

Figure 7-3: Network with redundant gateways

Next, we'll move on to the details of this setup. Just like in previous chapters, the baseline is an OpenBSD setup, but we note differences when dealing with other BSDs where relevant.

It's important to understand that the CARP addresses are virtual addresses. Unless you have console access to all machines in your CARP group, you will almost always want to assign an IP address to the physical interfaces in order to be able to communicate with the host and be absolutely sure which machine you are interacting with.

By convention, the IP address assigned to the physical interface will belong in the same subnet as the virtual, shared IP address. In fact, the kernel will by default try to assign the CARP address to a physical interface that is already configured with an address in the same subnet as the CARP address. You can override this interface selection by specifying a different interface in the `carpdev` option in the `ifconfig` command string you use to set up the CARP interface.

NOTE *When you are reconfiguring your network and the default gateway address becomes a virtual address instead of being fixed to a specific interface and host, it's extremely hard to avoid temporary loss of connectivity.*

Setting Up CARP: Kernel Options, sysctl, and ifconfig Commands

Most of the work in getting a redundant setup going lies in cabling, setting sysctl values, and issuing `ifconfig` commands. We describe the cabling only in the most general terms (and the main schematic comes naturally from the illustration or a corresponding one for your own setup). However, on some systems you will need to check that your kernel is set up with the required devices compiled in. Operating system–specific instructions are shown here.

OpenBSD users

Both the `carp` and `pfsync` devices are in the default *GENERIC* and *GENERIC.mp* kernel configurations. Unless you are running with a custom kernel and you removed these options, no kernel reconfiguration is necessary.

FreeBSD users

Check that your kernel has the `carp` and `pfsync` devices compiled in. The *GENERIC* kernel does not contain these options by default. See the *FreeBSD Handbook* for information on how to compile and install a custom kernel with these options.

NetBSD users

Check that your kernel has pseudo-device `carp` compiled in. NetBSD's default *GENERIC* kernel configuration does not have `carp` compiled in. However, you will find the relevant line commented out in the *GENERIC* configuration file. NetBSD does not yet support `pfsync`, because of protocol-numbering issues that were unresolved at the time this chapter was written.

On all CARP-capable systems, the basic functions are governed by a handful of sysctl variables. The main one, `net.inet.carp.allow`, is on by default. On a typical OpenBSD system you will see

```
$ sysctl net.inet.carp.allow
net.inet.carp.allow=1
```

which means that your system comes equipped for CARP.

If your kernel is not configured with a CARP device, issuing this command will instead produce something like sysctl: unknown oid 'net.inet.carp.allow' *on FreeBSD or* sysctl: third level name 'carp' in 'net.inet.carp.allow' is invalid *on NetBSD.*

To check that your system is set up properly, you could use this sysctl command to view all carp-related variables:[4]

```
$ sysctl net.inet.carp
net.inet.carp.allow=1
net.inet.carp.preempt=0
net.inet.carp.log=0
net.inet.carp.arpbalance=0
```

The important variables are the first two, while you will normally not need to touch the last two. For reference, setting net.inet.carp.log to 1 gives you debug information about the CARP traffic you logged, but this is turned off by default. Similarly the net.inet.carp.arpbalance variable can be used to enable CARP *arp balancing*, which offers some limited load balancing between hosts on a local network. However, for graceful failover between the gateways in the setup we are planning, we need to set the net.inet.carp.preempt variable:

```
$ sudo sysctl net.inet.carp.preempt=1
```

Setting the net.inet.carp.preempt variable means that on hosts with more than one network interface, such as our gateways, all CARP interfaces will set their advskew (the meaning of which we will explain more thoroughly in a moment) to the extremely high value of 240 in order to prod other hosts in the CARP group to start failover when one of the interfaces goes down. This setting needs to be identical on all hosts in the CARP group. When setting up your system, you need to repeat the setting on all hosts.

Next, you set up the network interfaces. Looking at the network diagram, we see that the local network uses addresses in the 192.168.12.0 network, while the external, Internet-facing interface is in the 192.0.2.0 network. With these address ranges and the CARP interface's default behavior in mind, the commands for setting up the virtual interfaces come naturally.

On the machine you want to set up as the initial master for the group, use these commands:

```
$ sudo ifconfig carp0 192.0.2.19 vhid 1
$ sudo ifconfig carp1 192.168.1.1 vhid 2
```

Note that we do not need to set the physical interface explicitly. The carp0 and carp1 virtual interfaces here will bind themselves to the physical interfaces that are already configured with addresses in the same subnets as

---

[4] On FreeBSD, you will also encounter the variable net.inet.carp.suppress_preempt, which is a read-only status variable indicating whether or not preemption is possible.

the assigned CARP address. With `ifconfig` you should be able to check that each CARP interface is properly configured:

```
$ ifconfig carp0
carp0: flags=8843<UP,BROADCAST,RUNNING,SIMPLEX,MULTICAST> mtu 1500
        lladdr 00:00:5e:00:01:01
        carp: MASTER carpdev ep0 vhid 1 advbase 1 advskew 0
        groups: carp
        inet 192.0.2.19 netmask 0xffffff00 broadcast 192.0.2.255
        inet6 fe80::200:5eff:fe00:101%carp0 prefixlen 64 scopeid 0x5
```

The `ifconfig` output for the other CARP interfaces will be quite similar to this. Note the `carp:` line, which indicates `MASTER` status. On the backup, the setup is almost identical, except that you add the `advskew` parameter:

```
$ sudo ifconfig carp0 192.0.2.19 vhid 1 advskew 100
$ sudo ifconfig carp1 192.168.1.1 vhid 2 advskew 100
```

The `advskew` parameter requires a bit of explanation. In short, it indicates how much *less preferred* it is for the specified machine to take over for the current master. The longer explanation is that `advskew` and its companion value `advbase` are used to calculate the interval between the current host's announcements of its master status when it has taken over. The default value for `advbase` is `1`; for `advskew` the default value is `0`. In our example, the master would announce every second $(1 + 0/256)$, while the backup would wait for $1 + 100/256$ seconds. With `net.inet.carp.preempt=1`, when the master stops announcing or announces it is not available, the backups will take over, and the new master will start announcing at its configured rate. Smaller `advskew` values mean shorter announcement intervals and higher likelihood for becoming the new master. If more hosts have the same `advskew`, the one that is already master will keep its master status.

From OpenBSD 4.1 onward, there is one more factor to the equation that determines which hosts takes over CARP master duty. The *demotion counter* is a value each CARP host announces for its `carp` interface group as a measure of readiness for its CARP interfaces. When the demotion counter value is zero, the host is in complete readiness, while higher values indicate measures of degradation. You can set the demotion counter from the command line using `ifconfig -g`, but the value is usually set by the system itself, with higher values typically set during the boot process. All other things being equal, the host with the lowest demotion counter will win the contest to take over as the CARP master.

On the backup, you once again use `ifconfig` to check that each CARP interface is properly configured:

```
$ ifconfig carp0
carp0: flags=8843<UP,BROADCAST,RUNNING,SIMPLEX,MULTICAST> mtu 1500
        lladdr 00:00:5e:00:01:01
        carp: BACKUP carpdev ep0 vhid 1 advbase 1 advskew 100
        groups: carp
        inet 192.0.2.19 netmask 0xffffff00 broadcast 192.0.2.255
        inet6 fe80::200:5eff:fe00:101%carp0 prefixlen 64 scopeid 0x5
```

Here the output is only slightly different; note that the carp: line here indicates BACKUP status along with the advbase and advskew parameters.

For actual production use, you will want to add a measure of security against unauthorized CARP activity by configuring the members of the CARP group with a shared, secret passphrase, such as

```
$ sudo ifconfig carp0 pass mekmitasdigoat 192.0.2.19 vhid 1
$ sudo ifconfig carp1 pass mekmitasdigoat 192.168.1.1 vhid 2
```

with your own choice of passphrase.[5] Just like any other password, the passphrase will then be a required ingredient in all CARP traffic in your setup, so take care to configure all CARP interfaces in a failover group with the same passphrase or none.

Once you have figured out the settings you want, you will preserve them through future system reboots by putting the settings in the proper files in */etc*: On OpenBSD, you put the proper `ifconfig` parameters into *hostname.carp0* and *hostname.carp1*; on FreeBSD and NetBSD, you put the relevant lines in your *rc.conf* file as contents of the `ifconfig_carp0=` and `ifconfig_carp1=` variables.

Keeping States Synced: Adding pfsync

The final piece of the puzzle before looking at the rule set itself is to configure state table synchronization between the hosts in your redundancy group. With synchronized state tables on the redundant firewalls, in almost all cases the traffic will see no disruption at all during failover. As we've hinted at earlier, the tool you need is a set of properly configured pfsync interfaces.

NOTE   *Because of protocol-numbering issues that were unresolved at the time this chapter was written, NetBSD unfortunately does not currently support pfsync.*

---

[5] This particular passphrase, however, has a very specific meaning. A web search will reveal its significance and why it is de rigueur for modern networking documentation. Or, if you're lazy, look it up at *http://marc.info/?l=openbsd-misc&m=98027812528843&w=2.*

Configuring pfsync interfaces is a matter of some planning and a few fairly straightforward ifconfig commands. It is possible to set up pfsync on any configured network interface, but it is generally a better idea to set up a separate network for the synchronization.

In our sample configuration (see Figure 7-3) we have set aside a tiny network for this purpose. Here, a crossover cable connects the two Ethernet interfaces, but in configurations with more than two hosts in the failover group, you may want to set up with a separate switch, hub, or vlan.

In this sample configuration, the interfaces we are planning to use for the synchronization have already been assigned IP addresses, 10.0.12.16 and 10.0.12.17, respectively. With the basic TCP/IP configuration done already, the complete pfsync setup for each of the two synchronization partner interfaces is

```
$ sudo ifconfig pfsync0 syncdev ep2
```

which illustrates the advantage of having identical hardware configurations as well as keeping pfsync traffic on a physically separate network.

The pfsync protocol itself offers little in the way of security features. It has no authentication mechanism and by default communicates via IP multicast traffic. However, for the cases where a physically separate network is not a feasible option, you can tighten up your pfsync security in two ways: by setting up pfsync to synchronize only with a specified syncpeer

```
$ sudo ifconfig pfsync0 syncpeer 10.0.12.16 syncdev ep2
```

and by protecting the sync traffic by using IPsec

```
$ sudo ifconfig pfsync0 syncpeer 10.0.12.16 syncdev enc0
```

which means that the syncdev device becomes the enc0 encapsulating interface instead of the physical interface.

NOTE   *If possible, set up your synchronization to happen across a physically separate, dedicated network.*

This takes us to the end of the basic network configuration for CARP-based failover. In the next section, we'll consider what you need to keep in mind when writing rule sets for redundant failover configurations.

Putting Together a Rule Set

After all the contortions we've been through in order to get the basic networking configured, you are probably wondering what it will take to migrate the rules you have put in your current *pf.conf* to the new setup.

The answer is, not very much. The main change you have introduced is essentially invisible to the rest of the world, and a well-designed rule set for a single gateway configuration will generally work well for a redundant setup, too. However, you have introduced two additional protocols, CARP and pfsync, and in all likelihood, you will need to make some relatively minor changes to your rule set in order to let the failover work properly.

Pass CARP traffic on the appropriate interfaces.

The most readable way is to introduce a macro definition for your carpdevs and an accompanying pass rule, such as

```
pass on $carpdevs proto carp keep state
```

Pass pfsync traffic on the appropriate interfaces.

The most readable way is to introduce a macro definition for your syncdev and an accompanying pass rule, such as

```
pass on $syncdev proto pfsync
```

or, if you want to take the pfsync device out of the filtering equation altogether, use

```
set skip on $syncdev
```

Also, you should consider the roles of the virtual CARP interface and its address versus the physical interface. As far as PF is concerned, all incoming traffic will come through the physical interfaces, but the traffic may have the CARP interface's IP addresses as source or destination addresses.

It may not always be necessary to synchronize every rule in your configuration (i.e., connections to services that run on the gateway itself) in case of a failover. One prime example would be the typical rule to allow ssh in for the administrator:

```
pass in on $int_if from $ssh_allowed to self
```

For those rules, you could use the state option no-sync to prevent synchronizing state changes for connections that are really not relevant after the failover has happened:

```
pass in on $int_if from $ssh_allowed to self keep state (no-sync)
```

With this configuration in hand, you will be able to schedule operating system upgrades and similar former downtime-producing activities on members of your carped group of systems when they are convenient to the system administrator, with no measurable or noticeable downtime for users of your services.

8

LOGGING, MONITORING, AND STATISTICS

Exercising control over a network, whether at home or at work, is probably a main objective for anyone who reads this book. One necessary element of keeping control is having access to all relevant information about what happens in your network. Fortunately for us, PF (like most components of Unix-like systems) is able to generate log data for network activity.

PF offers a wealth of options for setting the logging detail level, processing log files, and extracting specific kinds of data. You can already do a lot with the tools that are in your base system, but there are several other tools available via your BSD package system that you can use to collect, study, and present log data in a number of useful ways. In this chapter we'll take a closer look at PF logs in general and some of the tools you can use to extract and present useful information.

PF Logs: The Basics

What data PF records in the logs and at what level of detail is up to you, as determined by your rule set. The principle is simple: For each rule you want log data for, you add the log keyword.

When you load the rule set with log added to one or more rules, any packet that starts up a connection matching the rule (that is, blocked or passed) is copied to a pflog device.

PF will also store some additional data such as the timestamp, interface, whether the packet was blocked or passed, and the associated rule number from the loaded rule set. The PF log data is then collected by the pflogd logging daemon, which is started by default when PF is enabled at system startup. The default location for storing the log data is */var/log/pflog*; however, the log is written in the binary format used by tcpdump.[1]

To get started, let's take a look at a basic log example. Start with the rules you want to log, and add the log keyword:

```
block log all
pass log quick proto { tcp, udp } from any to any port ssh
```

Reload the rule set, and you will see the timestamp on your */var/log/pflog* file change as the file starts growing. To see just what data is being stored there, you can use tcpdump with the -r option to read the file.

If the logging has been going on for a while, typing

```
$ sudo tcpdump -n -ttt -r /var/log/pflog
```

on a command line can produce large amounts of output. The following sequence is just the first few lines of output from tcpdump that was several screens long, with almost all lines long enough to wrap:

```
$ sudo tcpdump -n -ttt -r /var/log/pflog
tcpdump: WARNING: snaplen raised from 96 to 116
Sep 13 13:00:30.556038 rule 10/(match) pass in on epic0: 194.54.107.19.34834 >
194.54.103.66.113: S 3097635127:3097635127(0) win 16384 <mss 1460,nop,nop,sackOK,nop,wscale
0,[|tcp]> (DF)
Sep 13 13:00:30.556063 rule 10/(match) pass out on fxp0: 194.54.107.19.34834 >
194.54.103.66.113: S 3097635127:3097635127(0) win 16384 <mss 1460,nop,nop,sackOK,nop,wscale
0,[|tcp]> (DF)
Sep 13 13:01:07.796096 rule 10/(match) pass in on epic0: 194.54.107.19.29572 >
194.54.103.66.113: S 2345499144:2345499144(0) win 16384 <mss 1460,nop,nop,sackOK,nop,wscale
0,[|tcp]> (DF)
Sep 13 13:01:07.796120 rule 10/(match) pass out on fxp0: 194.54.107.19.29572 >
194.54.103.66.113: S 2345499144:2345499144(0) win 16384 <mss 1460,nop,nop,sackOK,nop,wscale
0,[|tcp]> (DF)
Sep 13 13:01:15.096643 rule 10/(match) pass in on epic0: 194.54.107.19.29774 >
194.54.103.65.53: 49442 [1au][|domain]
Sep 13 13:01:15.607619 rule 12/(match) pass in on epic0: 194.54.107.19.29774 >
194.54.107.18.53: 34932 [1au][|domain]
```

---

[1] Additional tools to extract and display information from your log file will be discussed later. Rest assured, it's a well-documented and widely supported binary format.

You will find that `tcpdump` is a very flexible program, especially when it comes to output, providing a number of display choices. The format in this example follows quite straightforwardly from the options we fed to `tcpdump`. The program almost always displays the date and time the packet arrived (here, the -ttt option specifies long format). Next, `tcpdump` lists the rule number in the loaded rule set and the interface the packet appeared on, and then it lists the source and target address and ports (the -n option tells tcpdump to display IP addresses, not hostnames). Last, you'll see various packet properties. You will find the exact set of options that are the most useful for your purpose by reading the man page for `tcpdump`.

DECIPHERING RULE NUMBERS

It is worth noting that the rule numbers in your log files refer to the *loaded, in-memory* rule set. Your rule set goes through some automatic steps during the loading process, such as macro expansion and optimizations that make it very likely that the rule number as stored in the logs does not quite match what you would find by counting from the top of your *pf.conf* file. If it isn't immediately obvious to you which rule matched, you can find out by using the command `pfctl -vvs rules` (or `pfctl -vvsr`, if you want to save some typing) and studying the output.

In the example we just gave, the tenth rule in the loaded rule set seems to be a catch-all rule that matches both IDENT requests and domain name lookups. This is the kind of output you will find invaluable when debugging, and it is in fact fairly essential to have this kind of data at hand to stay on top of what is happening in your network. With a little effort and careful reading of the `tcpdump` man pages, you should be able to extract any log data you will find useful.

If you want a live display of the traffic you log, you can use `tcpdump` to read log information directly from the log device itself. To do this, use the -i command-line option to specify which interface you want `tcpdump` to read from, but the rest of the command is clearly recognizable:

```
$ sudo tcpdump -nettti pflog0
tcpdump: WARNING: pflog0: no IPv4 address assigned
tcpdump: listening on pflog0, link-type PFLOG
Sep 13 15:26:52.122002 rule 17/(match) pass in on epic0: 91.143.126.48.46618 >
194.54.103.65.22: [|tcp] (DF)
Sep 13 15:28:02.771442 rule 12/(match) pass in on epic0: 194.54.107.19.8025 >
194.54.107.18.8025: udp 50
Sep 13 15:28:02.773958 rule 10/(match) pass in on epic0: 194.54.107.19.8025 >
194.54.103.65.8025: udp 50
Sep 13 15:29:27.882888 rule 10/(match) pass in on epic0: 194.54.107.19.29774 >
194.54.103.65.53:[|domain]
Sep 13 15:29:28.394320 rule 12/(match) pass in on epic0: 194.54.107.19.29774 >
194.54.107.18.53:[|domain]
```

The output format is recognizable, too. This sequence starts off with an ssh connection. The next two connections are spamd synchronizations, followed by two domain name lookups. If you leave this command running, the displayed lines will eventually scroll off the top of your screen, but it is of course possible to redirect the data to a file or to a separate program for further processing.

NOTE *In some situations, you will be interested mainly in traffic to or from specific hosts or traffic matching other identifiable criteria that are narrower than the scope of the rules you log. For these situations, tcpdump's own filtering features can be useful in order to extract the data you need. See man tcpdump for details.*

Logging All Packets: log (all)

For most debugging and at least lightweight monitoring purposes, logging the first packet in a connection provides enough information. However, from time to time you may want to log all packets matching the rules you are interested in. You accomplish that by using the (all) logging option in the rules you want to monitor. After making this change to our minimal rule set, it looks like this:

```
block log (all) all
pass log (all) quick proto tcp from any to any port ssh keep state
```

This makes the logs quite a bit more verbose. To illustrate just how much more data log (all) generates, here is a different rule set fragment that passes domain name lookups and network time synchronizations:

```
udp_services = "{ domain, ntp }"
pass log (all) inet proto udp from any to any port $udp_services
```

With log (all) in the above rule, the following sequence shows what happens when a Russian nameserver sends a domain name request to one of my servers:

```
$ sudo tcpdump -n -ttt -i pflog0 port domain
tcpdump: WARNING: pflog0: no IPv4 address assigned
tcpdump: listening on pflog0, link-type PFLOG
Sep 30 14:27:41.260190 212.5.66.14.53 > 194.54.107.19.53:[|domain]
Sep 30 14:27:41.260253 212.5.66.14.53 > 194.54.107.19.53:[|domain]
Sep 30 14:27:41.260267 212.5.66.14.53 > 194.54.107.19.53:[|domain]
Sep 30 14:27:41.260638 194.54.107.19.53 > 212.5.66.14.53:[|domain]
Sep 30 14:27:41.260798 194.54.107.19.53 > 212.5.66.14.53:[|domain]
Sep 30 14:27:41.260923 194.54.107.19.53 > 212.5.66.14.53:[|domain]
```

That's six entries instead of just one. Even with everything except port domain filtered out by tcpdump in our example, it goes pretty much without saying that adding log (all) to one or more rules will increase the amount of data in the logs considerably. If your gateway's storage capacity is limited and you need to log all traffic, you may find yourself shopping for additional storage devices.

Logging to Several pflog Interfaces

In PF versions older than OpenBSD 4.1, only one pflog interface was available. That changed in OpenBSD 4.1, when the pflog interface became a *cloneable* device. This change means you can use ifconfig commands to create several pflog interfaces, in addition to the default pflog0. This in turn makes it practical to record the log data for different parts of your rule set to separate pflog interfaces. It also makes it easier to process the resulting data separately, if necessary.

The required changes to your setup are subtle but effective. In order to log to several interfaces, you need to make sure that all the log interfaces your rule set uses are created before the rule set is loaded. If your rule set logs to an interface that does not exist, the log data is simply discarded.

While you are in the process of tuning your setup for using several pflog interfaces, you will most likely add the required interfaces from the command line, such as

```
$ sudo ifconfig create pflog1
```

for as many pflog interfaces are required. You then specify the log device when you add the log keyword to your rule set, as follows:

```
pass log (to pflog1) proto tcp from any to $emailserver port $email
pass log (to pflog1) proto tcp from $emailserver to any port smtp
```

For a more permanent configuration on OpenBSD, you need to create a *hostname.pflog1* file that contains only

```
up
```

and similar *hostname.pflogN* files for any further logging interfaces you need.

On FreeBSD, the configuration of the cloned pflog interfaces belongs in your *rc.conf* file, where it turns up in the following form:

```
ifconfig_pflog1="up"
```

On NetBSD, cloning pflog interfaces was not an option at the time this book was written.

As we have seen already in Chapter 6, directing log information for different parts of your rule set to separate interfaces makes it possible to feed PF log data to separate applications. This in turn makes it easier to have programs such as spamlogd process only the relevant information while you feed other parts of your PF log data to other log-processing programs.

Logging to syslog, Local or Remote

One way to avoid storing PF log data on the gateway itself is to instruct your gateway to log to the system logs on another machine. If you already have a centralized logging infrastructure in place, it is a fairly logical thing to do, even if PF's ordinary logging mechanisms were not really designed with traditional syslog-style logging to a text file in mind.

A FEW WORDS OF CAUTION ABOUT SYSLOG

As any old BSD hand will tell you, it should be noted that the traditional syslog system log facility is a bit naïve about managing the data it receives over UDP from other hosts, with DoS attacks involving full disks as one frequently mentioned danger. There is also the ever-present risk that log information will be lost under a high load on either the systems or the network. For these reasons, you should consider setting up your system for remote logging *only* if all the hosts involved communicate over a well-secured network. On most BSDs, syslogd by default is not set up to accept log data from other hosts. See the syslogd man page for information about how to enable listening for log data from remote hosts if you plan to use remote syslog logging.

If this warning does not scare you away from doing your PF logging via syslog, here is a short recipe for how to do it.

In ordinary PF setups, pflogd handles the log data and copies the data to the log file. In a setup where you primarily want the log data to be stored on a remote system, you will want to disable pflog's data accumulation. You can do this by changing pflog's log file to */dev/null*, via the daemon's startup options in your *rc.conf.local* (on OpenBSD) to

```
pflogd_flags="-f /dev/null"
```

On FreeBSD and NetBSD, you change the pflog_logfile= line in *rc.conf* in a similar way, so it ends up looking like this:

```
pflog_logfile="/dev/null"
```

Then kill and restart the pflogd process with its new parameters.

The next step is to make sure that the log data, now no longer collected by pflogd, is transmitted in a meaningful way to your log-processing system instead. This has two parts: First, set up your system logger to transmit data to the log-processing system, and second, use tcpdump in tandem with logger to convert the data and inject it into the syslog system.

Setting up your syslogd to process the data is straightforward: Choose your *log facility*, *log level*, and *action*[2] and put the resulting line in your */etc/syslog .conf* file. Assuming you have already set up the system logger at *loghost .example.com* to receive your data and chosen log facility local2 with log level info, the correct line is

```
local2.info                        @loghost.example.com
```

After this change, you need to restart your syslogd to make it read the new settings. Then set tcpdump to convert the log data from the pflog device and feed the result to logger, which in turn sends the data to the system logger. Here we reuse the tcpdump command from the basic examples, with some useful additions:

```
$ sudo nohup tcpdump -lnettti pflog0 | logger -t pf -p local2.info &
```

The nohup command makes sure the process keeps running even if it does not have a controlling terminal or gets put in the background (as we do here with the trailing &). The -l option to tcpdump specifies line-buffered output, which is useful for redirecting to other programs, as we do here. At the other end of the pipe, logger adds the tag pf to identify the PF data in the stream and specifies log priority with the -p option as local2.info. The result is logged to the file you specify on the logging host, where the entries in the log file will look something like this:

```
pf: Sep 21 14:05:11.492590 rule 93/(match) pass in on ath0: 10.168.103.11.15842 >
82.117.50.17.80: [|tcp] (DF)
pf: Sep 21 14:05:11.492648 rule 93/(match) pass out on xl0: 194.54.107.19.15842 >
82.117.50.17.80: [|tcp] (DF)
pf: Sep 21 14:05:11.506289 rule 93/(match) pass in on ath0: 10.168.103.11.27984 >
82.117.50.17.80: [|tcp] (DF)
pf: Sep 21 14:05:11.506330 rule 93/(match) pass out on xl0: 194.54.107.19.27984 >
82.117.50.17.80: [|tcp] (DF)
pf: Sep 21 14:05:11.573561 rule 136/(match) pass in on ath0: 10.168.103.11.6430 >
10.168.103.1.53:[|domain]
pf: Sep 21 14:05:11.574276 rule 136/(match) pass out on xl0: 194.54.107.19.26281 >
209.62.178.21.53:[|domain]
```

The log fragment displayed here shows mainly web-browsing activities, with accompanying domain name lookups.

Tracking Statistics for Each Rule with Labels

The sequential information you get from retrieving log data basically tracks packet movements over time. In other contexts, the sequence or history of

---

[2] All of these concepts are explained very well in man syslog.conf, which is of course required reading if you want to understand system logs. The *action* part is usually a file in a local filesystem, as you will see from reading the configuration file and the man page.

connections is less important than aggregates such as the number of packets or bytes that have matched a rule since the counters were last cleared.

We have already seen how to use `pfctl -s all` to view the global aggregate counters along with a number of other data in "Statistics from pfctl" on page 15. If you want to see a more detailed breakdown of the data, you can keep track of traffic totals on a per-rule basis by using a slightly different form of the `pfctl` command, such as `pfctl -vs rules`, which displays statistics along with the rule:

```
$ pfctl -vs rules
pass inet proto tcp from any to 192.0.2.225 port = smtp flags S/SA keep state label "mail-in"
  [ Evaluations: 1664158   Packets: 1601986   Bytes: 763762591   States: 0     ]
  [ Inserted: uid 0 pid 24490 ]
pass inet proto tcp from 192.0.2.225 to any port = smtp flags S/SA keep state label "mail-out"
  [ Evaluations: 2814933   Packets: 2711211   Bytes: 492510664   States: 0     ]
  [ Inserted: uid 0 pid 24490 ]
```

The format is easy to read and obviously designed for contexts where you want to get an idea of what is going on with a simple glance.

On the other hand, the output from the previous command is not very well suited for feeding to a script or other program for further processing. If you want to extract these statistics and a few more items in a slightly more script-friendly format and make your own decisions about which rules are worth tracking, rule *labels* are for you.

Labels do more than identify rules for processing specific kinds of traffic. PF labels also make it easier to extract the traffic statistics. By attaching labels to rules, you store some extra data about parts of your rule set you are interested in or parts that require special attention. One good example of labeling is when you need to measure bandwidth use for accounting purposes.

Here we attach the labels `mail-in` and `mail-out` to our pass rules for incoming and outgoing mail traffic, respectively:

```
pass log proto { tcp, udp } from any to $emailserver port smtp label "mail-in"
pass log proto { tcp, udp } from $emailserver to any port smtp label "mail-out"
```

Some time after you have loaded the rule set with labels, you can check the data using the `pfctl -vsl` command:

```
$ sudo pfctl -vsl
mail-in 1664158 1601986 763762591 887895 682427415 714091 81335176
mail-out 2814933 2711211 492510664 1407278 239776267 1303933 252734397
```

The command output shows the label first, then the number of times the rule has been evaluated, followed by the total number of packets passed. The third value is the total number of bytes passed, followed by the number of packets passed in, the number of bytes passed in, the number of packets passed out, and finally the number of bytes passed out. While lacking in details for human consumption, this list format makes it very well suited for piping to and parsing by scripts and applications.

The counters run and accumulate from the time the rule set is initially loaded until they are reset. In many contexts it makes sense to set up a cron job that reads label values at fixed intervals and puts them in some sort of permanent storage. If you run the data collection at fixed intervals, it is worth considering collecting the data via pfctl -vszl instead. The z option resets the counters after pfctl has read them, and your data collector would then be fetching *periodic data,* or data accumulated since the last time the script was run.

NOTE   *It is worth noting that rules with macros and lists will expand to several distinct rules. If your rule set contains rules with lists and macros that then have a label attached, the in-memory result will be a number of rules, all with a separate, identically named label attached to it. While this may lead to confusing pfctl -vsl output, it is not really a problem as long as the application or script that receives the data is able to interpret the data correctly by adding up the totals for the identical labels.*

Some Additional Tools for PF Logs and Statistics

One other important component of staying in control of your network is having the ability to keep an updated view of your system's status. In this section we'll take a look at a selection of monitoring tools that you may find useful.

This is not a complete lineup of all the available tools that are capable of interacting with your PF configuration. However, all the tools presented here are available via the package system on OpenBSD and FreeBSD (and, with one exception, NetBSD).

Keeping an Eye on Things with pftop

If you are interested in keeping an eye on what passes in to and out of your network at the moment, Can Erkin Acar's pftop is a very useful tool. The name is a strong hint at what it does—pftop shows a running snapshot of your traffic in a format strongly inspired by the traditional Unix process viewer top.

This is a minimally edited screenshot of pftop running on one of my gateways:

```
pfTop: Up State 1-21/67, View: default, Order: none, Cache: 10000        19:52:28

PR   DIR SRC                   DEST                 STATE   AGE   EXP  PKTS BYTES
tcp  Out 194.54.103.89:3847    216.193.211.2:25     9:9     28    67    29  3608
tcp  In  207.182.140.5:44870   127.0.0.1:8025       4:4     15 86400    30  1594
tcp  In  207.182.140.5:36469   127.0.0.1:8025       10:10  418    75   810 44675
tcp  In  194.54.107.19:51593   194.54.103.65:22     4:4    146 86395   158 37326
tcp  In  194.54.107.19:64926   194.54.103.65:22     4:4    193 86243   131 21186
tcp  In  194.54.103.76:3010    64.136.25.171:80     9:9    154    59    11  1570
tcp  In  194.54.103.76:3013    64.136.25.171:80     4:4      4 86397     6  1370
tcp  In  194.54.103.66:3847    216.193.211.2:25     9:9     28    67    29  3608
tcp  Out 194.54.103.76:3009    64.136.25.171:80     9:9    214     0     9  1490
tcp  Out 194.54.103.76:3010    64.136.25.171:80     4:4     64 86337     7  1410
```

```
udp  Out  194.54.107.18:41423   194.54.96.9:53      2:1   36   0   2   235
udp  In   194.54.107.19:58732   194.54.103.66:53    1:2   36   0   2   219
udp  In   194.54.107.19:54402   194.54.103.66:53    1:2   36   0   2   255
udp  In   194.54.107.19:54681   194.54.103.66:53    1:2   36   0   2   271
```

You can sort your connections by a number of different criteria, among them by PF rule, volume, age, source and destination addresses, and a few other possibilities.

This program is not in the base system itself, probably because it is possible to extract equivalent information (although not quite in a real-time view) using various pfctl options. However, pftop is available as a package, in ports on OpenBSD and FreeBSD as *sysutils/pftop*, and on NetBSD via pkgsrc as *sysutils/pftop*.

Graphing Your Traffic with pfstat

Once you have a system up and running and producing data worth monitoring, graphs with curves representing traffic data are the hands-down favorite form of data representation. Fortunately, it is fairly easy to satisfy the demand for graphic representation of PF data.

One popular solution is pfstat, a small utility developed by Daniel Hartmeier to extract and present statistical data that is automatically generated by PF. The pfstat tool is available via the OpenBSD package system or as the port *net/pfstat*, via the FreeBSD ports system as *sysutils/pfstat*, and via NetBSD pkgsrc as *sysutils/pfstat*.

The program collects the data you specify in the configuration file and presents the data as JPG or PNG graphics files. The data source can be either PF running on the local system via the */dev/pf* device or data collected from a remote computer running the companion pfstatd daemon.

Setting up pfstat is mainly a matter of deciding which parts of your PF data you want to put together in a graph and how. You then write the configuration file and start cron jobs to collect the data and generate your graphs.

The program comes with a well-annotated sample configuration file and a brief but useful man page. The sample configuration is in fact a useful starting point for writing your own. I'll show you a small example.

The following *pfstat.conf* fragment is very close to one you will find in the sample configuration:[3]

```
collect  8 = global states inserts  diff
collect  9 = global states removals diff
collect 10 = global states searches diff

image "/var/www/users/peter/bsdly.net/pfstat-states.jpg" {
        from 1 days to now
        width 980 height 300
```

---

[3] The color values in the example give you a graph with red, blue, and green lines. For the monochrome print version, we changed the colors to grayscale values: 0 192 0 became 105 105 105, 0 0 255 became 192 192 192, and 255 0 0 became 0 0 0.

```
left
        graph 8 "inserts" "states/s" color 0 192 0 filled,
        graph 9 "removals" "states/s" color 0 0 255
    right
        graph 10 "searches" "states/s" color 255 0 0
}
```

Collecting state insertions, removals, and searches once a minute and then graphing the data collected over the last day to a JPG file produces a graph roughly like the one in Figure 8-1, with data from one of my less-busy gateways.

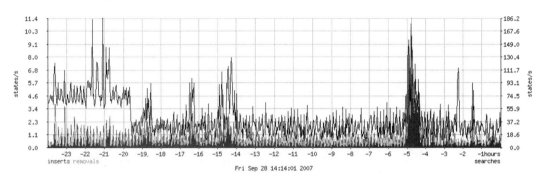

Figure 8-1: State table statistics, 24-hour time scale

For a more detailed view of the same data, I decided I wanted the data for the last hour, only in a slightly higher resolution. I changed the period to from 1 hours to now and the dimensions to width 600 height 300, producing the graph in Figure 8-2.

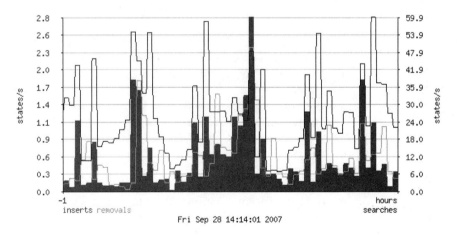

Figure 8-2: State-table statistics, 1-hour time scale

The `pfstat` home page at *http://www.benzedrine.cx/pfstat.html* contains a number of other examples, with demonstrations in the form of live updates of graphs that show data from the *benzedrine.cx* domain's gateways. By reading the examples and tapping your own knowledge of your traffic, you should be able to create `pfstat` configurations that are well suited to your site's needs.

Collecting NetFlow Data with pfflowd

NetFlow is a network data collection and analysis method that has spawned a large family of supporting tools for recording and analyzing data about TCP/IP connections. NetFlow originated at Cisco, and over time it has become supported in various network equipment as an important management-and-analysis feature.

If NetFlow tools are already part of your network toolset, it is useful and perhaps even crucial to know that PF data can be made available to NetFlow tools via the `pfflowd` package.

The NetFlow data model defines a *network flow* as a unidirectional sequence of packets with the same source and destination IP address and protocol. This maps very well to PF state information, and `pfflowd` is intended to record state changes from the local system's `pfsync` device. Once enabled, `pfflowd` acts as a NetFlow sensor that converts `pfsync` data to NetFlow format for transmission to a NetFlow collector on the network.

The `pfflowd` tool was written and is maintained by Damien Miller and is available from his website (*http://www.mindrot.org/projects/pfflowd*) as well as through the package systems on OpenBSD and FreeBSD as *net/pfflowd*. The lack of `pfsync` support on NetBSD means that `pfflowd` is not available on that platform at the time this book was written.

SNMP Tools and PF-Related SNMP MIBs

The Simple Network Management Protocol (SNMP) was designed to let network administrators collect and monitor key data about how their systems run and potentially change configurations on multiple network nodes from a centralized system.

The protocol debuted with RFC 1067 in August 1988 and is now in its third major version as defined in RFCs 3411 through 3418. The SNMP protocol comes with a well-defined interface and a method for extending the *Management Information Base (MIB)*, which defines the managed devices and objects.

SNMP manageability support has become such a required component in serious networking equipment that, if your network is large enough, you probably looked up this section before deciding whether this book was worth buying.

Network management and monitoring systems, both proprietary and open source, generally have SNMP support in one form or another, and in some products it's a core feature. On the BSDs, SNMP support has generally come in the form of the `net-snmp` package, which provides the tools you need to retrieve SNMP data and to collect data for retrieval by management systems. The package is available on OpenBSD as *net/net-snmp*, on FreeBSD as *net-mgmt/net-snmp*, and on NetBSD as *net/net-snmp*.

Fortunately, an extension to the net-snmp package that makes PF data available to SNMP monitoring is available, too. Joel Knight maintains MIBs for retrieving data on PF, CARP, and OpenBSD kernel sensors, download-able as patches to net-snmp from *http://www.packetmischief.ca/openbsd/snmp*.

After you install the package and the extension, your SNMP-capable monitoring systems will be able to watch PF data too, in any detail you could desire. In addition, it is worth noting that FreeBSD's bsnmpd includes a PF module. See the bsnmpd man page for details.

Remember, Useful Log Data Is the Basis for Effective Debugging

In this chapter we have walked through the basics of collecting, displaying, and interpreting data about a running system with PF enabled. Knowing how to find and use information about how your system behaves is helpful for several purposes.

Keeping track of the status of a running system is useful in itself, but the ability to read and interpret log data is even more essential for finding out whether your setup in fact behaves according to specifications. Another prime use for log data is tracking the effect of changes you make in the configuration, such as when tuning your system to give optimal performance.

Checking your configuration and tuning it for optimal performance, based on log data and other observations, is a large part of what we will be dealing with in the next chapter.

9

GETTING YOUR SETUP JUST RIGHT

By now you have spent a significant amount of time designing your network and implementing that design in your PF configuration. Getting your setup just right and removing any remaining setup bugs and inefficiencies can be quite challenging at times. In this chapter we'll discuss some options and methods that will help you get the setup you need. First, we'll take a look at global options and some settings that can have a profound influence on how your configuration behaves.

The Things You Can Tweak and What You Probably Should Leave Alone

Network configurations are inherently very tweakable. While browsing the *pf.conf* man page or other reference documentation, it is easy to be overwhelmed by the number of options and settings that you could adjust to get that perfectly optimized setup.

It is important to keep in mind that with PF, *the defaults are sane* for most setups. However, some settings and variables lend themselves to tuning, while others should come with a big warning that they should be adjusted to non-default values only in highly unusual circumstances. We will discuss some of these scenarios in this chapter.

Let's start by looking at some of the global settings that you may want to be aware of, but that you may not have to change at all under most circumstances. If you read man pf.conf, you will discover that there are a few other options available, but they're not particularly relevant in a network-testing and performance-tuning context.

The global options, which you write as set *option setting*, are placed after any macro definitions in your *pf.conf* but before translation or filtering rules. The following sections explain some examples.

block-policy

This option determines what feedback, if any, PF will give to hosts trying to create connections that are subsequently blocked. The option has two possible values: drop, which drops blocked packets with no feedback, and return, which returns with status codes such as Connection refused or something similar.

The correct strategy for block policies has been the subject of many discussions over the years. The default setting for block-policy is drop, which means that the packet is silently dropped without any feedback. However, silently dropping packets increases the likelihood that the sender will resend the unacknowledged packets rather than drop the connection. Thus, the effort is kept up until the relevant timeout counter expires. Unless you can think of a good reason to set it to something else, the recommendation is to set the block policy to return, as in

```
set block-policy return
```

which means that the sender's networking stack receives an unambiguous signal that the connection was refused. It's also worth noting that this setting specifies the *global* default for your block policy. If necessary, you can still vary the blocking type for specific rules.

You could, for example, change the brute force protection rule set from "Turning Away the Brutes" on page 68 to have block-policy set to return but use block drop quick from <bruteforce> to make the brute forcers waste some extra energy if they stay around after they have been added to the <bruteforce> table. Another example is dropping traffic from nonroutable addresses coming in on your Internet-facing interface.

skip

The skip option lets you exclude specific interfaces from all PF processing. The net effect is strikingly similar to a pass-all rule for the interface, such as pass on $int_if. One common example of explicit skip is to disable filtering on the loopback interface, where filtering in most configurations adds little security or convenience:

```
set skip on lo0
```

In fact, filtering on the loopback interface is almost never useful, and it could lead to odd results with a number of common programs and services. The default is that skip is unset, which means that all configured interfaces will potentially take part in PF processing. In addition to making your rule set slightly simpler, setting skip on interfaces where you do not want to perform filtering results in a slight performance gain.

state-policy

The state-policy option specifies how PF matches packets to the state table. The possible values are floating and if-bound. The differences between the two lie in how subsequent packets are treated once a state table entry has been created.

With the default floating state policy, traffic can match state on all interfaces, not just the interface where the state was created. With an if-bound policy, traffic will match only on the interface where the state is created. Traffic on other interfaces or groups will not match the existing state. Like block-policy, this option specifies the *global* state-matching policy. You can override state policy on a per-rule basis if needed. For example, in a rule set with the default floating state policy, you could have a rule like this:

```
pass out on egress inet proto tcp to any port $allowed modulate state (if-bound)
```

With this rule, any return traffic trying to pass back in would need to pass on the same interface where the state was created in order to match the state table entry.

WARNING *The situations in which state-policy if-bound is useful are rare enough that the general recommendation is to leave this setting at the default.*

timeout

The timeout option sets the timeouts and related options for various interactions with the state table entries. The majority of the parameters are protocol-specific values stored in seconds and prefixed tcp., udp., icmp., and other.. However, adaptive.start and adaptive.end denote the number of state table entries.

These options can be used for optimizing your setup for performance, but changing the protocol-specific settings from the default values creates a significant risk that valid but idle connections might be dropped prematurely or blocked outright.

The timeout options you are most likely to change are the following:

adaptive.start and adaptive.end

These values set the limits for scaling down timeout values once the number of state entries reaches the adaptive.start value. When the number of states reaches adaptive.end, all timeouts are set to zero, essentially expiring all states immediately. The default values are 6000 and 12000 (calculated as 80 percent and 120 percent of the state limit), respectively. These settings are intimately related to the memory pool limit parameters you set via the limit option discussed in the next section.

interval

This value denotes the number of seconds between purges of expired states and fragments. The default value is 10 seconds.

frag

The frag value denotes the number of seconds a fragment will be kept in an unassembled state before it is discarded. The default value is 30 seconds.

src.track

When set, src.track denotes the number of seconds source-tracking data will be kept after the last state has expired. The default value is 0 seconds.

You can inspect the current settings for all timeout parameters with pfctl -s timeouts. This display shows a system running with default values.

```
$ sudo  pfctl -s timeouts
tcp.first              120s
tcp.opening             30s
tcp.established      86400s
tcp.closing            900s
tcp.finwait             45s
tcp.closed              90s
tcp.tsdiff              30s
udp.first               60s
udp.single              30s
udp.multiple            60s
icmp.first              20s
icmp.error              10s
other.first             60s
other.single            30s
other.multiple          60s
frag                    30s
interval                10s
adaptive.start        6000 states
adaptive.end         12000 states
src.track               0s
```

limit

The limit option sets the size of the memory pools PF uses for state tables and address tables. These are hard limits, so you may need to increase or tune the values for a variety of reasons. If your network is a busy one with larger numbers than the default values allow, or if your setup requires large address tables or a large number of tables, then this section will be very relevant for you.

It is important to keep in mind that the total amount of memory available through memory pools is taken from the *kernel memory space*, and the amount available is a function of the total available kernel memory. The kernel allocates a fixed amount of memory for its own use at system startup; however, since kernel memory is never swapped, the amount of memory allocated for the kernel's own use can never equal or exceed the physical memory in the system. If that happened, there would be no space for user-mode programs to run. The exact amount of pool memory available depends on which hardware platform you use as well as on a number of hard-to-predict variables specific to the local system. On the i386 architecture the maximum kernel memory is in the 768MB to 1GB range, depending on a number of factors, including the exact number and kind of hardware devices in the system. The amount actually available for allocation to memory pools comes out of this total, again depending on a number of system-specific variables.

You can inspect the current limit settings using pfctl -sm. Typical output looks like this:

```
$ sudo pfctl -sm
states        hard limit    10000
src-nodes     hard limit    10000
frags         hard limit     5000
tables        hard limit     1000
table-entries hard limit   200000
```

To change these values, you edit your *pf.conf* to include one or more lines with new limit values. For example, you would use these lines to raise the hard limit for number of states to 25,000 and table entries to 300,000:

```
set limit states 25000
set limit table-entries 300000
```

You can also set several limit parameters at a time in a single line by enclosing them in brackets, like this:

```
set limit { states 25000, src-nodes 25000, table-entries 300000 }
```

In the end, you almost certainly should not change the limits at all. If you do, however, it is important to watch your system logs for any indication that your changed limits do not have undesirable side effects or do not fit in available memory. Setting the debug level to a higher value is potentially quite useful for watching the effects of tuning limit parameters.

debug

The debug option determines what, if any, error information PF will generate at the kern.debug log level. The default value is urgent, which means that only serious errors will be logged. The other possible settings are none (no messages), misc (reporting slightly more than urgent), and finally loud (producing status messages for most operations). After I ran my home gateway at debug level loud for a little while, this is what my */var/log/messages* file looked like:

```
$ tail -f /var/log/messages
Oct  4 11:41:11 skapet /bsd: pf_map_addr: selected address 194.54.107.19
Oct  4 11:41:15 skapet /bsd: pf: loose state match: TCP 194.54.107.19:25 194.54.107.19:25
158.36.191.135:62458 [lo=3178647045 high=3178664421 win=33304 modulator=0 wscale=1]
[lo=3111401744 high=3111468309 win=17376 modulator=0 wscale=0] 9:9 R seq=3178647045
(3178647044) ack=3111401744 len=0 ackskew=0 pkts=9:12
Oct  4 11:41:15 skapet /bsd: pf: loose state match: TCP 194.54.107.19:25 194.54.107.19:25
158.36.191.135:62458 [lo=3178647045 high=3178664421 win=33304 modulator=0 wscale=1]
[lo=3111401744 high=3111468309 win=17376 modulator=0 wscale=0] 10:10 R seq=3178647045
(3178647044) ack=3111401744 len=0 ackskew=0 pkts=10:12
Oct  4 11:42:24 skapet /bsd: pf_map_addr: selected address 194.54.107.19
```

As you can see, the loud level gives you a level of detail where PF repeatedly reports the IP address for the interface it is currently handling. In between the selected address messages, PF warns twice for the same packet that the sequence number is at the very edge of the expected range. This level of detail seems almost breathtaking at first glance, but in some circumstances studying this kind of output is the best way to diagnose a problem and later check to see if your solution actually helped.

It is worth noting that this option can be set from the command line with pfctl -x, followed by the debug level you want. The command pfctl -x loud gives you maximum debugging info, while pfctl -x none turns off debug messages entirely. Keep in mind that the output of the loud debug setting can be large amounts of data—and in extreme cases could impact performance all the way to self-DoS level.

ruleset-optimization

The ruleset-optimization option sets the mode for the rule set optimizer. The default is basic, which means that no automatic optimization is performed. If you include this line

```
set ruleset-optimization basic
```

in your *pf.conf* and reload your configuration, the rule set is subjected to some further processing before it loads.

With basic rule set optimization enabled, the optimizer does the following things:

•   Removes duplicate rules

- Removes rules that are subsets of other rules

  For example, say you have the macro `tcp_services = { ssh, www, https }` combined with the rule `pass proto tcp from any to self port $tcp_services`. Elsewhere in your rule set, you have a different rule that says `pass proto tcp from any to self port ssh`. The second rule is clearly a subset of the first, and they can be merged into one. Another common combination is having a `pass` rule like `pass proto tcp from any to int_if:network port $tcp_services` with otherwise identical `pass` rules where the target addresses are all in the `int_if:network` range.

- Merges rules into tables if appropriate

  Typical rule-to-table optimizations are rules that pass, redirect, or block based on identical criteria except source and/or target addresses.

- Changes rules order to improve performance

With rule set optimization set to `profile`, the optimizer analyzes the loaded rule set relative to the actual network traffic in order to determine the optimal order of `quick` rules.

You can also set the value of the optimization option from the command line with `pfctl`:

```
$ sudo pfctl -o basic
```

This example enables the rule set optimization in basic mode.

NOTE *Since the optimization may remove or reorder rules, the meaning of some statistics, mainly the number of evaluations per rule, may change in ways that are hard to predict. In most cases, however, the effect is negligible.*

optimization

The `optimization` option specifies profiles for state-timeout handling. The possible values are `normal`, `high-latency`, `satellite`, `aggressive`, and `conservative`. The recommendation is to keep the default `normal` setting unless you have very specific needs. The values `high-latency` and `satellite` are synonyms, where states expire more slowly in order to compensate for potential high latency. The `aggressive` setting expires states early in order to save memory (be forewarned, though, that you run the risk of dropping idle-but-valid connections if your system is already close to its load and traffic limits). Finally, the `conservative` setting goes to great length to preserve states and idle connections, at the cost of some additional memory use.

Cleaning Up Your Traffic: scrub and antispoof

The next two features we'll discuss, `scrub` and `antispoof`, share a common theme: They provide automated protection against potentially dangerous clutter in your network traffic. Together they are commonly referred to as tools for "network hygiene," because they sanitize your networking considerably.

scrub

The scrub keyword enables network traffic normalization. With scrub, fragmented packets are reassembled, and invalid fragments such as overlapping fragments are discarded, so the resulting packet is complete and unambiguous. Enabling scrub provides a measure of protection against certain kinds of attacks based on incorrect handling of packet fragments.[1] A number of supplementing options are available, but the simplest form shown here is suitable for most configurations:

```
scrub in all
```

In order for some services to work with scrub, specific options must be set. One commonly cited example is NFS, where some combinations of buggy clients and servers have been reported not to work with scrub at all unless you use the no-df parameter. Some combinations of services, operating systems, and network configurations may require more exotic scrub options. If you find yourself having to debug a scrub-related problem, you are well advised to study the *pf.conf* man page and consult the gurus on the relevant mailing lists.

antispoof

There are some very useful and common packet-handling actions that could be written as PF rules, but not without their becoming long, complicated, and error-prone rule set boilerplate. Thus, antispoof was implemented for a common special case of filtering and blocking. This mechanism protects against activity from spoofed or forged IP addresses, mainly by blocking packets that appear on interfaces traveling in directions that are not logically possible.

With antispoof, we can specify that we want to weed out spoofed traffic coming in from the rest of the world and any spoofed packets that (however unlikely) were to originate in our own network. Figure 9-1 illustrates the concept.

To establish the kind of protection depicted in the diagram, specify antispoof for both interfaces in the illustrated network with these two lines:

```
antispoof for $ext_if
antispoof for $int_if
```

These lines in turn expand to complex rules. The first one, for instance, blocks incoming traffic when the source address appears to be part of the network directly connected to the antispoofed interface but arrives on a

---

[1] Some notable attack techniques, including several now-historical Denial of Service (DoS) setups, have exploited bugs in fragment handling that could lead to out-of-memory conditions or other resource exhaustion. One such exploit, which was aimed at Cisco's PIX firewall series, is described in the advisory at *http://www.cisco.com/en/US/products/products_security_advisory09186a008011e78d.shtml.*

different interface. However, `antispoof` is not designed to detect address spoofing remotely for networks that are not directly connected to the machine running PF.

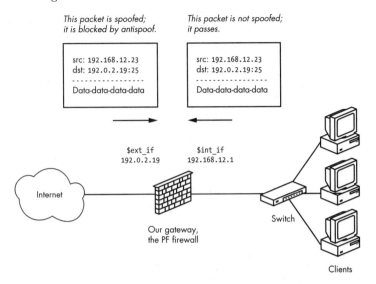

Figure 9-1: *antispoof drops packets that come in from the wrong network.*

Testing Your Setup

Now that we have set our focus on testing, it's time to dust off the precise specification that describes how your setup *should* work. We put it aside for a few chapters in order to show you the features we thought you would like to know about, but now it's pretty essential that you have your specification ready for referencing. Realistically, for anything past a truly trivial setup, it is fairly essential to have a specification in hand.

The specification we have been working through in this book runs roughly like this, with minor variations:

The physical layout of our sample network is centered on a *gateway* that is connected to the Internet via $ext_if. Attached to the gateway via $int_if is a *local network* with workstations and possibly one or more servers for local use. Finally, we have a *DMZ* connected to $dmz_if, populated with servers offering services to the local network and the Internet. Figure 9-2 shows the logical layout for the network.

The corresponding rule set specification looks something like this:

- Machines outside our network should have access to the services offered by our servers in the DMZ and no access at all to the local network.

- The machines in our local network, attached to $int_if, should have access to the services offered by the servers in the DMZ as well as access to a defined list of services outside our network.

- The machines in the DMZ should have access to some network services in the outside world.

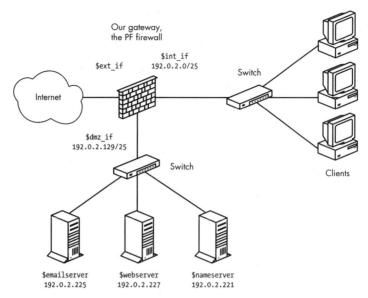

Figure 9-2: Network with servers in a DMZ

The task at hand, then, is to make sure the rule set we have in place actually implements the specification. We need to test the setup. A useful test would be to try the sequence in Table 9-1.

Table 9-1: Sample Rule Set Test Case Sequence

Test Action	Expected Result
Try a connection from the local network to each of the allowed ports on the servers in the DMZ.	The connection should pass.
Try a connection from the local network to each of the allowed ports on servers outside our network.	The connection should pass.
Try a connection on any port from the DMZ to the local network.	The connection should be blocked.
Try a connection from the DMZ to each of the allowed ports on servers outside our network.	The connection should pass.
Try a connection from outside our network to $webserver in the DMZ on each of the ports in $webports.	The connection should pass.
Try a connection from outside our network to $webserver in the DMZ on port 25 (SMTP).	The connection should be blocked.
Try a connection from outside our network to $emailserver in the DMZ on port 80 (HTTP).	The connection should be blocked.
Try a connection from outside our network to $emailserver in the DMZ on port 25 (SMTP).	The connection should pass.
Try a connection from outside our network to one or more machines in the local network.	The connection should be blocked.

Your configuration may call for other tests or could differ in some particulars. It is likely that your real-life test scenario should specify how packets and connections should be logged. The important thing is that you decide what is the expected and desired result for each of your test cases before you start testing.

In general, you should test using the applications you expect the typical user to have, such as web browsers or mail clients on various operating systems. The connections should simply succeed or fail, according to specifications. If one or more of your basic tests gives an unexpected result, you move on to *debugging* your rule set.

Debugging Your Rule Set

What happens when your configuration does not behave as you expected it to? It is possible there is an error in the rule set's logic, and if so you need to find the error and correct it. Tracking down logic errors in your rule set can be time consuming and could involve manually evaluating your rule set, both as it is stored in the *pf.conf* file and the loaded version after macro expansions and any optimizations.

Before diving into the rule set itself, you can easily determine whether the PF configuration is what is causing the problem. Disabling PF by running the command pfctl -d to see if the problem disappears is a valid test that can save you a lot of trouble.

On the mailing lists, news groups, and other forums, we frequently see users initially blaming PF for problems that turn out to be basic network problems. Network interfaces set to the wrong duplex settings, bad netmasks, or even faulty network hardware are common culprits.

If the problem persists when PF is not enabled, it is likely that the problem is not in the PF configuration. You should then turn to debugging other parts of your network configuration instead. However, if you are about to start adjusting your PF configuration, it is worth checking that PF is in fact enabled and that your rule set is loaded, using the following command:

```
$ sudo pfctl -si | grep Status
Status: Enabled for 20 days 06:28:24          Debug: Loud
```

Here Status: Enabled tells us that PF is enabled, so we try viewing the loaded rules with a different pfctl command:

```
$ sudo pfctl -sr
scrub in all fragment reassemble
block return log all
block return log quick from <bruteforce> to any
anchor "ftp-proxy/*" all
```

Here, `pfctl -sr` is equivalent to `pfctl -s rules`. The actual output is likely to be a bit longer than what we show here, but it's a good example of what you should expect to see when a rule set is definitely loaded. For debugging purposes it is useful to add the -vv flag to the `pfctl` command line to see rule numbers and some additional debug information, like this:

```
$ sudo pfctl -vvsr
@0 scrub in all fragment reassemble
  [ Evaluations: 67274995  Packets: 34231784  Bytes: 9800756925 States: 0    ]
  [ Inserted: uid 0 pid 1013 ]
@0 block return log all
  [ Evaluations: 618114    Packets: 15833     Bytes: 1444217    States: 0    ]
  [ Inserted: uid 0 pid 1013 ]
@1 block return log quick from <bruteforce:2> to any
  [ Evaluations: 618114    Packets: 13208     Bytes: 792140     States: 0    ]
  [ Inserted: uid 0 pid 1013 ]
@2 anchor "ftp-proxy/*" all
  [ Evaluations: 604906    Packets: 3498832   Bytes: 2803255822 States: 0    ]
  [ Inserted: uid 0 pid 1013 ]
```

At this time, you should perform a structured walkthrough of the loaded rule set. Find the rules that match the packets you are investigating. What is the last matching rule? If more than one rule matches, is one of the matching rules a quick rule?[2] You will need to trace the evaluation until you hit the end of the rule set or until the packet matches a quick rule, which then ends the process. If your rule set walk-through ends somewhere other than with the rule you were expecting to match your packet, you have found your logic error.

Rule set logic errors tend to fall into three types of cases:

- Your rule does not match because it is never evaluated. A quick rule earlier in the rule set matched, and the evaluation stopped.

- Your rule is evaluated but does not match the packet after all because of the rule's criteria.

- Your rule is evaluated, the rule matches, but the packet also matches another rule later in the rule set. The last matching rule is the one that determines what happens to your connection.

In Chapter 8 we introduced `tcpdump` as a valuable tool for reading and interpreting PF logs. The program is also very well suited for viewing what traffic passes on a specific interface. What you learned about PF's logs and how to use `tcpdump`'s filtering features will come in handy when you want to track down exactly which packets reach which interface.

---

[2] As you probably recall from earlier chapters, when a packet matches a quick rule, evaluation stops and whatever the quick rule specifies is what happens to the packet.

Here we use `tcpdump` to watch for TCP traffic on the xl0 interface (but not show SSH or SMTP traffic) and print the result in very verbose mode (vvv).

```
$ sudo tcpdump -nvvvpi xl0 tcp and not port ssh and not port smtp
tcpdump: listening on xl0, link-type EN10MB
21:41:42.395178 194.54.107.19.22418 > 137.217.190.41.80: S [tcp sum ok]
3304153886:3304153886(0) win 16384 <mss 1460,nop,nop,sackOK,nop,wscale 0,nop,nop,timestamp
1308370594 0> (DF) (ttl 63, id 30934, len 64)
21:41:42.424368 137.217.190.41.80 > 194.54.107.19.22418: S [tcp sum ok]
1753576798:1753576798(0) ack 3304153887 win 5792 <mss 1460,sackOK,timestamp 168899231
1308370594,nop,wscale 9> (DF) (ttl 53, id 0, len 60)
```

The connection shown here is a successful connection to a website.

There are more interesting things to look for, though, such as connections that fail when they should not, according to your specification, or connections that succeed when your specification says they clearly should not.

The test in these cases involve tracking the packets' path through your configuration. Once more, it is useful to check to see if PF is enabled or if disabling PF makes a difference. Building on the result from that initial test, you then perform the same kind of analysis of the rule set as we described previously. Once you have a reasonable theory of how the packets should traverse your rule set and your network interfaces, use `tcpdump` to see the traffic on each of the interfaces in turn. Use `tcpdump`'s filtering features to see only the packets that should match your specific case, such as `port smtp` and `dst 192.0.2.19`.

Find the exact place where your assumptions no longer match the reality of your network traffic. Turn on logging for the rules that may be involved, and then turn `tcpdump` loose on the relevant `pflog` interface to see which rule the packets actually match.

The main outline for the test procedure is fairly fixed. If you have narrowed down the cause to your PF configuration, once more it's a case of finding out which rules match and which rule ends up determining whether the packet passes or is blocked.

Know Your Network, Stay in Control

The recurring theme in this book has been how PF and related tools make it relatively easy for you, as the network administrator, to take control of your network and make it behave the way you want it to. In other words, this book is about building the network you need.

Running a network can be fun, and I hope you have enjoyed this tour of what I consider to be the best tool available. In presenting PF, I made a conscious decision early on to introduce you to its methods and ways of thinking via interesting and useful configurations, rather than make this book *the complete reference*. The complete PF reference already exists in the man pages, which are updated every six months with the new OpenBSD releases. Following this chapter you will find a list of online and print literature I have found useful, with short comments for each entry, followed by a note on hardware, various kinds of support, and how to interact with the developer and user communities.

Now that you have a basic knowledge of what PF can do, you can start building networks according to your own ideas of what you need in each case. It's all up to you, and now you will see that you have reached the point where you can find your way around the man pages and locate the exact information you need. This is when the fun part starts!

A

RESOURCES

These resources should help you get the most out of your setup. Though I wanted to, it proved impossible to cover all possible wrinkles of PF configuration; I hope that the resources listed here will fill in some details or present a slightly different perspective. Some of them are even quite enjoyable reads for their own sake. Hopefully most of the resources listed here will remain useful and updated.

General Networking and BSD Resources on the Internet

These are the general web-accessible resources cited throughout the book. It is worth looking at the various BSD projects' websites for the most up-to-date information.

- Of particular interest for OpenBSD users is the online *OpenBSD Journal* (*http://undeadly.org*). It offers news and articles about OpenBSD and related issues.

- OpenBSD's website (*http://www.openbsd.org*) is the main reference for OpenBSD information. If you're using OpenBSD, you will be visiting this site every now and then.

- You will find a collection of presentations and papers by OpenBSD developers at *http://www.openbsd.org/papers*. This site is a good source of information about ongoing developments in OpenBSD.

- OpenBSD's *Documentation and Frequently Asked Questions* (*http://www.openbsd.org/faq/index.html*) is more of a user guide than a traditional question-and-answer document. This is where you'll find a generous helping of background information and stepwise instructions on how to set up and run your OpenBSD system.

- *PF: The OpenBSD Packet Filter* (*http://www.openbsd.org/faq/pf/index.html*) is the official PF documentation, maintained by the OpenBSD team. The PF user guide gets updated for each release and is an extremely valuable reference resource for PF practitioners.

- Bob Beck's "pf. It's not just for firewalls anymore" (*http://www.ualberta.ca/~beck/nycbug06/pf*) is a NYCBUG 2006 presentation that covers PF's redundancy and reliability features, with real-world examples taken from the University of Alberta network.

- Daniel Hartmeier's PF pages (*http://www.benzedrine.cx/pf.html*) are his collection of PF-related material with links to resources around the Web.

- Daniel Hartmeier's "Design and Performance of the OpenBSD Stateful Packet Filter (pf)" (*http://www.benzedrine.cx/pf-paper.html*) is the paper he presented at USENIX 2002, which describes the initial design and implementation of PF.

- Daniel Hartmeier's three-part *undeadly.org* PF series, from September 2006, was originally intended as chapters for a book that was unfortunately canceled. This series of articles comprises "PF: Firewall Ruleset Optimization" (*http://undeadly.org/cgi?action=article&sid=20060927091645*); "PF: Testing Your Firewall" (*http://undeadly.org/cgi?action=article&sid=20060928081238*); and "PF: Firewall Management" (*http://undeadly.org/cgi?action=article&sid=20060929080943*). The three articles cover their respective subjects in great detail, yet manage to be quite readable.

- RFC 1631, "The IP Network Address Translator (NAT)," May 1994, (*http://www.ietf.org/rfc/rfc1631.txt?number=1631*) is the first part of the NAT specification, which has proved to be longer lived than the authors had apparently intended. While still an important resource for understanding NAT, it has been largely superseded by the updated RFC 3022, dated January 2001.

- RFC 1918, "Address Allocation for Private Internets," February 1996, (*http://www.ietf.org/rfc/rfc1918.txt?number=1918*) is the second part of the NAT and private address space puzzle. This RFC describes the motivations for the allocation of private, nonroutable address space and defines the address ranges. RFC 1918 has been designated a Best Current Practice.

Sample Configurations and Related Musings

A number of people have been kind enough to write up their experiences and make sample configurations available on the Web. The following are some of my favorites.

- Marcus Ranum's "The Six Dumbest Ideas in Computer Security" (*http://www.ranum.com/security/computer_security/editorials/dumb/index.html*), from September 2005, is a longtime favorite of mine. This article explores some common misconceptions about security and their unfortunate implications for real-world security efforts.

- Nate Underwood's "HOWTO: Transparent Packet Filtering with OpenBSD" (*http://ezine.daemonnews.org/200207/transpfobsd.html*), from 2002, shows a filtering bridge configuration.

- Randal L. Schwartz's "Monitoring Net Traffic with OpenBSD's Packet Filter" (*http://www.samag.com/documents/s=9053/sam0403j/0403j.htm*) shows a real-life example of traffic monitoring and using labels for accounting. Some details about PF and labels have changed in the intervening years, but the article is still quite readable and presents several important concepts well.

- The Swedish user group Unix.se's "Brandvägg med OpenBSD" (*http://unix.se/Brandv%E4gg_med_OpenBSD*) and its sample configurations, such as the basic ALTQ configurations, were quite useful to me early on. The site serves as a nice reminder that volunteer efforts such as local user groups can be excellent sources of information.

- Randal L. Schwartz's blog for Thursday, January 29, 2004 (*http://use.perl.org/~merlyn/journal/17094*) shows how he apparently solved an annoying problem via creative use of ALTQ and operating system fingerprinting.

- Kenjiro Cho's "Managing Traffic with ALTQ" (*http://www.usenix.org/publications/library/proceedings/usenix99/cho.html*) is the original ALTQ paper, which describes the design and the early implementation on FreeBSD.

- Jason Dixon's "Failover Firewalls with OpenBSD and CARP," from *SysAdmin Magazine*, May 2005 (*http://www.samag.com/documents/s=9658/sam10505e.html*) is an overview of CARP and pfsync, with some practical examples.

- Theo de Raadt's OpenCON 2006 presentation, "Open Documentation for Hardware: Why hardware documentation matters so much and why it is so hard to get" (*http://openbsd.org/papers/opencon06-docs/index.html*) was an important inspiration for the note in Appendix B about hardware for free operating systems in general and OpenBSD in particular.

PF on Other BSD Systems

PF has been ported from OpenBSD to the other BSDs, and while the stated goal for these efforts is, naturally, to be as up to date as possible in relation to the newest PF versions coming out of OpenBSD, it is useful to keep track of the PF projects in the other BSDs.

The "FreeBSD packet filter (pf)" home page (*http://pf4freebsd.love2party .net*) describes the early work with PF on FreeBSD and the project goals. At the moment the page is not quite up to date with the latest developments, but it will hopefully spring to life again once Max Laier notices that he's referenced in a book.

Peter Postma's "PF Loadable Kernel Module for NetBSD 2" (*http://nedbsd .nl/~ppostma/pf*) has patches and documentation for PF on NetBSD, including some of the relatively recent features that are not yet integrated in the main NetBSD tree.

BSD and Networking Books

In addition to what appears to be an ever-expanding number of online resources, there are several books that may be useful as companions or supplements to this book.

- Jacek Artymiak, *Building Firewalls with OpenBSD and PF*, 2nd ed. (devGuide .net, 2003). Traditionally *the* recommended PF book, it covers PF in OpenBSD 3.4 in great detail.

- Michael W. Lucas, *Absolute OpenBSD* (No Starch Press, 2003). Written at the time of OpenBSD 3.4, this volume offers a thorough walkthrough of OpenBSD with a wealth of hands-on, practical material.

- Brandon Palmer and Jose Nazario, *Secure Architectures with OpenBSD* (Addison-Wesley, 2004). This book provides an overview of OpenBSD's features with a marked slant toward building secure and reliable systems. The book references OpenBSD 3.4 as the then up-to-date version.

- Douglas R. Mauro and Kevin J. Schmidt, *Essential SNMP*, 2nd ed. (O'Reilly Media, 2005). As the title says, this is an essential reference book about SNMP.

- Jeremy C. Reed (editor), *The OpenBSD PF Packet Filter Book* (Reed Media Services, 2006). The book is based on the *PF User Guide*, extended to cover PF on FreeBSD, NetBSD, and DragonFly BSD, and with some additional material on third-party tools that interoperate with PF.

Wireless Networking Resources

Kjell Jørgen Hole's Wi-Fi courseware (*http://www.kjhole.com/Standards/WiFi/WiFiDownloads.html*) is an excellent resource for understanding wireless networks. The courseware is mainly aimed at University of Bergen students who take Professor Hole's courses, but it is freely available and well worth reading.

For keeping up with developments in the wireless networking world, the WNN Wi-Fi Net News site offers running updates, with the security-related stories listed at *http://wifinetnews.com/archives/cat_security.html*.

Another highly recommended resource for wireless security issues is "The Unofficial 802.11 Security Web Page" (*http://www.drizzle.com/~aboba/IEEE*).

spamd and Greylisting-Related Resources

If handling email and dealing with email problems is part of your life (or is likely to be in the future), you have probably enjoyed the description of spamd, tarpitting, and greylisting. If you want a little more background information than what you find in the relevant RFCs, the following documents and Web resources provide it.

- The Greylisting.org website (*http://www.greylisting.org*) contains a useful collection of greylisting-related articles and other information about greylisting and SMTP in general.

- Evan Harris's "The Next Step in the Spam Control War: Greylisting" (*http://greylisting.org/articles/whitepaper.shtml*) is the original greylisting paper.

- Bob Beck's "OpenBSD spamd—greylisting and beyond" (*http://www.ualberta.ca/~beck/nycbug06/spamd*) is an NYCBUG presentation that explains how spamd works, leading up to a description of spamd's role in University of Alberta's infrastructure. It is worth noting that much of the *future work* mentioned in the presentation has already been implemented.

- Peter N.M. Hansteen's "The Silent Network: Denying the spam and malware chatter using free tools" (*http://home.nuug.no/~peter/malware-talk/silent-network.pdf*) is my BSDCan 2007 paper, a best-practice description of how to use greylisting, spamd, and various other free tools and OpenBSD to successfully fight spam and malware in your network.

Book-Related Web Resources

For news and updates about this book, book-related downloads, and errata, first check the book's home page at the No Starch Press website (*http://www.nostarch.com/pf.htm*). That page contains links to pages on my personal web space, where various updates and book-related resources will appear as they become available. I will be posting book-related news and updates at *http://www.bsdly.net/bookofpf*.

I maintain the PF tutorial manuscript, "Firewalling with OpenBSD's PF packet filter," which is the forerunner of this book. My policy is to make updates when appropriate, usually as I become aware of changes or features of PF and related software and while preparing for appearances at conferences. The tutorial manuscript is available under a BSD license and can be downloaded in several formats from my web space at *http://home.nuug.no/~peter/pf*. Updated versions will appear at that URL more or less in the natural course of tinkering in between events.

If You Enjoyed This Book, Buy OpenBSD CDs and Donate!

If you have enjoyed this book or found it useful, please go to the OpenBSD.org "Ordering" page at *http://www.openbsd.org/orders.html* and buy CD sets or, for that matter, support further development work by the OpenBSD project with a donation, such as via the "Donations" page at *http://www.openbsd.org/donations.html*.

If you are the kind of corporate entity that is more comfortable with donating to a corporation, you can contact the OpenBSD Foundation, a Canadian nonprofit corporation that was created in 2007 for that specific purpose. See the OpenBSD Foundation website at *http://www.openbsdfoundation.org* for more information.

If you've found this book at a conference, there might even be an OpenBSD booth nearby where you can buy CDs, T-shirts, or other items.

Remember, even free software takes real work and real money to develop and maintain.

B

A NOTE ON HARDWARE SUPPORT

How's the hardware support? I tend to hear that a lot, and my answer usually runs like this: In my experience, OpenBSD and other free systems tend to just work.

But for some reason, there is a general perception that going with free software means picking hardware components that will actually work will be a serious struggle.

There may be a factual basis for some of this—I certainly remember struggling with FreeBSD 2.0.5, which managed to boot its installer off the CD but was unable to actually complete an install since the CD drive I had was not supported.

But wait—that was back in *June 1995*.

If you do not remember that far back, this was when PC CD drives more often than not came with an almost-but-not-quite-IDE interface, attached to the sound card (or *multimedia package*) the drive came bundled with. At least that's what I had at the time. The BSDs came more from a *real-computer* or, in modern terms, *server* perspective, so SCSI and the like were better supported, and asking for help in a BSD-related newsgroup produced comments about "seriously losing hardware"—hackerspeak of the time for equipment that is just too badly designed or too primitive to be worth a hacker's time.

True enough, and around that time, cheap PCs generally did not come with networking circuitry built in, either. Configuring a network usually meant moving jumpers around on the network interface card or the motherboard itself or running some weird proprietary setup software. That is, if you had the good luck to be on something with an Ethernet interface. Dial-up and ISDN were more likely connections to the Internet back then.

Today you can reasonably expect all important components in your system to work with OpenBSD. Some caution and a bit of planning may be required for building the optimal setup, but wouldn't you rather plan and design your infrastructure carefully than shop by momentary impulse and hope for the best?

A Case in Point: The Story of a Small Wireless Network

Wireless network support in OpenBSD, and BSDs in general, is getting better all the time, but this does not mean that getting all the bits you need is necessarily easy.

A brief history of the wireless setup for my home network goes like this: I started out buying two CNet CWP-854 cards, which should have been supported in OpenBSD 3.7 via the new ral driver. The one I put in the brand-new Dell machine running a non-free operating system worked right out of the box. My gateway, however, which had been running without incident since the 3.3 days, was a little more problematic. The card was recognized and configured, but once the Dell tried to get an IP address, the gateway went down with a kernel panic. The gory details are available as OpenBSD PR 4217. I promised to test the card again with a new snapshot as soon as I could re-locate the card.[1]

I then decided I wanted to try ath cards and bought a D-Link DWL-G520, which I somehow managed to misplace while moving. Next, I bought a DWL-G520+, thinking that the plus sign must mean it's better. Unfortunately, the plus sign meant a whole different chipset was used, the TI ACX111, which comes with a low price tag but with no documentation accessible to free software developers. Fortunately, the store let me return the card for a refund with no trouble at all.

At this point, I was getting rather frustrated and went all the way across town to a shop that had several DWL-AG520 cards in stock. They were a bit more expensive than the others, but the card did work right away. A couple of weeks later the G520 turned up, and of course that worked, too. My laptop (which at the time ran FreeBSD) came with a Realtek 8180 wireless mini-PCI card built in, but for some reason I could not get it to work. I ended up buying a DWL-AG650 CardBus card, which works flawlessly with the ath driver.

---

[1] More than two years of deadline chasing later, the card is most likely still in one of the boxes we packed for the move. I hope I will locate the right box while PCI cards are still useful.

More than two years later, the acx driver (introduced in OpenBSD 4.0) brought reverse-engineered support for ACX1nn-based cards to the BSDs. It took quite a while and significant effort, and the development happened against the stated wishes of the vendor, but that's a theme we'll explore in "Issues Facing Hardware-Support Developers" on page 144. The point here is that there's value in careful planning.

Getting the Right Hardware

Getting the right hardware is essentially a matter of checking that what is supported in your system meets the needs of your network. It's always good practice to check the hardware compatibility lists at your operating system's website. You could also check the man pages or use apropos *keyword* commands (where *keyword* is the type of device you are looking for). Searching the archives of relevant mailing lists is also useful if you feel you need more background information.

You should be aware, though, that some hardware comes with odd restrictions. One such example is hardware that depends on firmware that is loaded onto the card. Often in these situations, the manufacturer refuses to grant redistribution rights for the firmware, and operating systems such as OpenBSD can't package it with their releases.

Laptops provide an excellent example of this situation. If you have shopped around for laptops recently, you've likely looked at units that come with Intel PRO/Wireless 3945ABG 802.11a/b/g networking hardware. That hardware is quite popular and supported in a wide range of operating systems, including OpenBSD via the wpi(4) driver. However, the hardware does not work at all unless you have the correct firmware files on your system, which Intel requires that you download from its site along with a license agreement.

This means that OpenBSD, despite its excellent support for network installs, cannot be installed over a wireless network on laptops with this particular Intel PRO/Wireless hardware. After all, Intel has refused to give permission to include the necessary files on the install media.

In the case of the wpi driver and firmware, reading the driver man page will reveal that the driver's maintainer has collected the firmware files and made an installable package of them. You can download the package file from his web space, which kind of feels like cheating (I'm not sure it is strictly legal with respect to the license agreement), but installing the package does solve the problem.

This Intel PRO/Wireless chipset is not the only device with such restrictions, but it happens to be what came with my ThinkPad R60, which is an otherwise excellent system. It is worth noting that in cases where supported hardware is restricted like this, the OpenBSD man pages tend to note the fact and in some cases even include the email addresses of people who might be in a position to change the manufacturer's policy.

My general advice is this: If you shop online, keep the man pages available in another tab or window, and if you go to a physical store, make sure to tell the clerks you will be using a BSD. If you're not sure about the parts they are trying to sell you, see if you can borrow a machine to browse the man pages and other documentation online. Telling the clerks up front could end up making it easier to get a refund if the part does not work, and telling them the part *did* work is good advocacy.

Issues Facing Hardware-Support Developers

Systems such as OpenBSD and the other BSDs did not spring fully formed from the forehead of a deity (although some will argue that the process was not, in fact, that different). Rather, they're the result of years of effort by a number of smart and dedicated individuals known as developers.

The developers are all highly qualified and extremely dedicated people who work tirelessly—the majority in their spare time—to produce amazing results. However, they do not live in a bubble with access to everything they need. Either the hardware itself or adequate documentation to support it is often unavailable to them. Another common problem is documentation that is provided only under a nondisclosure agreement, which limits how developers can use the information.[2]

Through a process called *reverse engineering*, developers can write drivers to support hardware even without proper documentation, but it is a complicated process of educated guessing, coding, and testing. It can be fun if you know how to do it, but it also has its own problems: It takes a long time to do, and, for reasons known only to lawmakers and lobbyists, it has legal consequences in several jurisdictions around the world.

So what's a soul to do in order to help the developers get the hardware and other material they need?

How to Help the Hardware-Support Efforts

If you are able to contribute quality code, the BSD projects are likely to welcome your contribution. If you are not a developer yourself, contributing code may not be an option, but there are several things you can do even if you are not a coder:

Buy your hardware from open source–friendly vendors.
If you are making decisions or recommendations when it comes to your organization's equipment purchases, it is well worth telling potential suppliers that *open source friendliness* is a factor in your purchasing decision.

---

[2] This is a frequent talk topic too; see, for example, Theo de Raadt's OpenCON 2006 presentation, "Open Documentation for Hardware: Why hardware documentation matters so much and why it is so hard to get," available at *http://www.openbsd.org/papers/opencon06-docs/index.html.*

Let the hardware vendors know what you think about their support (or lack thereof) for your favorite operating system.

Some hardware vendors have been quite helpful, supplying both sample units and programmer documentation. Others have been less forthcoming and some downright hostile toward developers asking for sample units and/or documentation. Both kinds of vendors, and the ones somewhere in between, need the right kind of encouragement. Write to them, and tell them what you think they are doing right and what they can do to improve. If, for example, a vendor has refused to make programming documentation available, or available only under a nondisclosure agreement (NDA), a reasoned, well-formulated letter from a potential customer could be what makes the vendor start cooperating.

Help test the system, and check out the drivers for hardware you are interested in.

If a driver exists or is in the process of being developed, the developers are generally insatiable for reports on how their code behaves on other people's equipment. Reports that the system is working fine are always appreciated, but bug reports with detailed descriptions of what goes wrong are actually even more essential to creating and maintaining a high-quality system.

Donate hardware or money.

The developers can always use hardware to develop on and money for day-to-day needs. If you are in a position to donate money or hardware, check out the projects' donations or items-needed pages. For OpenBSD, the URL for the donations page is *http://www.openbsd.org/donations.html,*[3] while specific equipment needs are listed at *http://www.openbsd.org/ want.html.* Donating to OpenBSD is what is most likely to help PF development along, but if you prefer to donate to FreeBSD, NetBSD, or DragonFly BSD instead, you will be able to find information on how to contribute financially to those projects at their respective websites.

Whatever your relationship with the BSDs and your hardware, I hope this helps you make intelligent decisions about what to buy and how to interact with both computers and people. And hopefully, the rest of the book will also help you improve your interactions with computers and people.

---

[3] If you are the kind of corporate entity that is more comfortable with donating to a corporation, you can contact the OpenBSD foundation, a Canadian nonprofit corporation that was created in 2007 for that specific purpose. See the OpenBSD Foundation website at *http://www .openbsdfoundation.org* for more information.

INDEX

R

Raadt, Theo de, 2
Random Early Detection (RED), 90
Ranum, Marcus, 13
rc scripts, 9–11, 20
rc system, 8
rdr rule, 25
RED (Random Early Detection), 90
redirection
    address pools, 50–51
    hoststated, 51–65
    load balancing and, 50–51, 57
    local networks and, 58–59
    NAT, 57
    round robin, 50–51
    web traffic, 43–44
redundancy, 97–105
Reed, Darren, 1–2
relay definition, 55
resources, 135–140
return value, 122
reverse engineering, 144
RFC 1067, 118
RFC 1631, 5
RFC 1918, 5
RFC 2018, 55
RFC 2821, 75–76
round-robin option, 51
routable addresses, 3, 26, 46–51
rule editor, xvii, 7
rule numbers, 109, 132
rule sets
    access points, 38–39
    blocking incoming/outgoing
        traffic, 13–15
    CARP traffic, 104–105
    debugging, 131–133
    default, 8, 9
    default deny, 13
    lists, 13–15, 115
    loading, 14
    logic errors, 131–132
    macros, 13–15, 21, 23, 115
    managing, xvi
    minimal, 12, 110
    optimizing, 126–127
    pfsync traffic, 98, 104–105
    putting together, 104
    readability of, 19
    restrictive, 13–15
    sample, xvii
    services by name in, 13
    simple, 11–12
    single, stand-alone machine, 11–15
    syntax errors in, 14
    testing, 12, 129–131
rules
    editing, xvii, 7
    evaluation order, 11, 22, 127
    flushing, 14
    labels, 113–115
    log data for. *See* log files; logging
    merging into tables, 127
    specific rules for gateways, 18–19
    statistics for, 113–115
    subsets, 127
    tracking statistics for, 113–115
ruleset-optimization option, 126–127

S

scp tool, 24
SCP transfers, 93–94
scrub keyword, 19, 127–128
Secure Shell protocol (SSH), 39,
        68–70
    traffic, 93
    transfers, 93
security
    attacks on. *See* attacks
    CARP and, 103–104
    FTP and, 24
    IPv6 and, 5
    local networks and, 48
    NAT and, 6
    network services, 16
    wireless networks, 34, 40–44
servers
    in DMZ, 49–50, 94–96
    fileservers, 46–51
    FTP, 26, 27
    load balancing, 50–51
    on local network, 46–48
    mail servers, 46–51, 56–59
    master/slave, 46
    nameservers, 46, 48
    queuing for, 94–96
    SMTP, 83–84
    webservers, 46–51, 56–59

THE OpenBSD FOUNDATION
A Canadian Not-for-Profit Corporation

OpenBSD · OpenSSH · OpenBGPD · OpenNTPD · OpenCVS

The OpenBSD Foundation exists to support OpenBSD—the home of pf—and related projects. While the OpenBSD Foundation works in close cooperation with the developers of these wonderful free software projects, it is a separate entity.

If you use pf in a corporate environment, please point management to the URL below, and encourage them to contribute financially to the Foundation.

www.OpenBSDFoundation.org

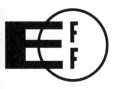

Electronic Frontier Foundation
Defending Freedom in the Digital World

Free Speech. Privacy. Innovation. Fair Use. Reverse Engineering. If you care about these rights in the digital world, then you should join the Electronic Frontier Foundation (EFF). EFF was founded in 1990 to protect the rights of users and developers of technology. EFF is the first to identify threats to basic rights online and to advocate on behalf of free expression in the digital age.

The Electronic Frontier Foundation Defends Your Rights!
Become a Member Today!
http://www.eff.org/support/

Current EFF projects include:

Protecting your fundamental right to vote. Widely publicized security flaws in computerized voting machines show that, though filled with potential, this technology is far from perfect. EFF is defending the open discussion of e-voting problems and is coordinating a national litigation strategy addressing issues arising from use of poorly developed and tested computerized voting machines.

Ensuring that you are not traceable through your things. Libraries, schools, the government and private sector businesses are adopting radio frequency identification tags, or RFIDs – a technology capable of pinpointing the physical location of whatever item the tags are embedded in. While this may seem like a convenient way to track items, it's also a convenient way to do something less benign: track people and their activities through their belongings. EFF is working to ensure that embrace of this technology does not erode your right to privacy.

Stopping the FBI from creating surveillance backdoors on the Internet. EFF is part of a coalition opposing the FBI's expansion of the Communications Assistance for Law Enforcement Act (CALEA), which would require that the wiretap capabilities built into the phone system be extended to the Internet, forcing ISPs to build backdoors for law enforcement.

Providing you with a means by which you can contact key decision-makers on cyber-liberties issues. EFF maintains an action center that provides alerts on technology, civil liberties issues and pending legislation to more than 50,000 subscribers. EFF also generates a weekly online newsletter, EFFector, and a blog that provides up-to-the minute information and commentary.

Defending your right to listen to and copy digital music and movies. The entertainment industry has been overzealous in trying to protect its copyrights, often decimating fair use rights in the process. EFF is standing up to the movie and music industries on several fronts.

Check out all of the things we're working on at http://www.eff.org and join today or make a donation to support the fight to defend freedom online.

ELECTRONIC FRONTIER FOUNDATION · 454 SHOTWELL STREET · SAN FRANCISCO, CA 94110 · 415.436.9333

HACKING, 2ND EDITION
The Art of Exploitation

by JON ERICKSON

While other books merely show how to run existing exploits, *Hacking: The Art of Exploitation* broke ground as the first book to explain how hacking and software exploits work and how readers could develop and implement their own. In the second edition, author Jon Erickson again uses practical examples to illustrate the most common computer security issues in three related fields: programming, networking, and cryptography. All sections have been extensively updated and expanded, including a more thorough introduction to the complex, low-level workings of a computer. Readers can easily follow along with example code by booting the included LiveCD, which provides a Linux programming environment and all of its benefits without the hassle of installing a new operating system.

DECEMBER 2007, 480 PP. W/CD, $49.95
ISBN 978-1-59327-144-2

SILENCE ON THE WIRE
A Field Guide to Passive Reconnaissance and Indirect Attacks

by MICHAL ZALEWSKI

Silence on the Wire: A Field Guide to Passive Reconnaissance and Indirect Attacks explains how computers and networks work, how information is processed and delivered, and what security threats lurk in the shadows. No humdrum technical white paper or how-to manual for protecting one's network, this book is a fascinating narrative that explores a variety of unique, uncommon, and often quite elegant security challenges that defy classification and eschew the traditional attacker-victim model.

APRIL 2005, 312 PP., $39.95
ISBN 978-1-59327-046-9

SECURITY DATA VISUALIZATION
Graphical Techniques for Network Analysis

by GREG CONTI

Security Data Visualization is a well-researched and richly illustrated introduction to the field of information visualization, a branch of computer science concerned with modeling complex data using interactive images. Greg Conti, creator of the network and security visualization tool RUMINT, shows you how to graph and display network data using a variety of tools so that you can understand complex datasets at a glance. And once you've seen what a network attack looks like, you'll have a better understanding of its low-level behavior—like how vulnerabilities are exploited and how worms and viruses propagate.

SEPTEMBER 2007, 272 PP., 4-COLOR, $49.95
ISBN 978-1-59327-143-5

ABSOLUTE FREEBSD, 2ND EDITION

The Complete Guide to FreeBSD

by MICHAEL W. LUCAS

Absolute FreeBSD, 2nd Edition is the newly updated edition of the best-selling and highly regarded guide to FreeBSD, now covering version 7.0. Written by FreeBSD committer Michael W. Lucas with the help and advice of dozens of FreeBSD developers, *Absolute FreeBSD, 2nd Edition* covers installation, networking, security, network services, system performance, kernel tweaking, filesystems, SMP, upgrading, crash debugging, and much more.

NOVEMBER 2007, 744 PP., $59.95
ISBN 978-1-59327-151-0

BUILDING A SERVER WITH FREEBSD 7

by BRYAN J. HONG

The most difficult aspect of building a server (to act as a fileserver, webserver, or mail server) is the initial software installation and configuration. *Building a Server with FreeBSD 7* tackles the problem systematically, so you can accomplish the task yourself efficiently and affordably using the freely licensed FreeBSD operating system. This book includes clear and straightforward instructions for installing and setting up everything you might like to run on your server.

FEBRUARY 2008, 256 PP., $34.95
ISBN 978-1-59327-145-9

PHONE:
800.420.7240 OR
415.863.9900
MONDAY THROUGH FRIDAY,
9 A.M. TO 5 P.M. (PST)

FAX:
415.863.9950
24 HOURS A DAY,
7 DAYS A WEEK

EMAIL:
SALES@NOSTARCH.COM

WEB:
WWW.NOSTARCH.COM

MAIL:
NO STARCH PRESS
555 DE HARO ST, SUITE 250
SAN FRANCISCO, CA 94107
USA

UPDATES

Visit *http://www.nostarch.com/pf.htm* for updates, errata, and other information.

COLOPHON

The fonts used in *The Book of PF* are New Baskerville, Futura, and Dogma.
    The book was printed and bound at Malloy Incorporated in Ann Arbor, Michigan. The paper is Glatfelter Thor 60# Antique, which is made from 15 percent postconsumer content. The book uses a RepKover binding, which allows it to lay flat when open.